Tunisia

WILFRID KNAPP

with 27 illustrations and 3 maps

WALKER AND COMPANY
NEW YORK

© Wilfrid Knapp 1970

Library of Congress Catalog Card Number: 68-13998

First published in the United States of America in 1970 by the Walker Publishing Company, Inc.

Printed in Great Britain by Hazell Watson & Viney Ltd, Aylesbury, Bucks

Contents

1   Nation and land

WHAT MAKES A NATION? The question admits of no simple
answer, whether in theory or in practice. In countries a century old,
like Canada and Belgium, nationhood is still fragile; a fair proportion of new states are riven by civil war – and the experience of
China suggests that the illness may be chronic. In other countries
nationalism strangles nationhood by its strident intolerance.

A sense of nationhood derives from awareness of past importance
and continuing traditions, from a common language and a sense of
a way of life. It flourishes best in the absence of deep internal divisions
caused by tribal allegiance, diversity of language or religious differences. A nation remains free from the strident self-destructive force
of overweening nationalism if it enjoys self-confidence, if it is not
beset by ambitions towards hegemony or by a hankering after some
past age of ancient grandeur.

Tunisians have achieved unity as a nation in a way others have
not. But the Tunisian example does not fit neatly into any precon-
ceived generalization, nor does it provide a classic case against which
other examples of nationhood may be measured. It has the unique
experience of the leadership of Bourguiba and a system which he
has established. In a real sense Bourguiba has created modern
Tunisia; yet great as his achievements are, they would not have
produced nationhood of the kind now to be found in Tunisia had
they not met with responsiveness from the Tunisians.

Past greatness is evident throughout Tunisia; and great monuments do much to enhance the self-respect of a nation. They are not
memorials to an antique Tunisian state, for such did not exist –

fortunately perhaps, since the medieval kingdoms of Bohemia, Croatia or Poland were most often a source of intellectual irrelevance or illusory importance in the nationalism of eastern Europe.

Carthage is one such monument – although the least spectacular in its physical remains. Originally an outpost of the Phoenician empire, it achieved greatness in its own right and became the most threatening, though in the end unsuccessful, rival to imperial Rome – which built on its ashes. Carthage continues to evoke grandeur and splendour. The French built their proud cathedral on the hill overlooking Tunis; its sad shell still bears the inscription: *Ab ipsis ecclesiae Africanae primordiis praestitisse Carthaginem nemo dubitat.* On the seashore beside the ruins of the Antonine baths stands the presidential palace where Bourguiba is most often in residence. The history of Carthage, Punic and Roman alike, contains its fair share of warfare, cruelty, greed and lust. Its smaller relics include votives of Tanit, the goddess to whom infants were sacrificed, and Roman lamps showing the delights of love which the French White Fathers excavated and placed in their museum. But legend, like the human psyche from which it is born, is kind to the past. Today Carthage evokes grandeur and a sense of importance in world history – as anyone may know who travels on that most unpretentious of all railways, the TGM from Tunis to La Marsa, and stops at the several Carthage stations.

The grace of Roman Carthage is preserved in its mosaics, while for spectacular Roman ruins one must go to Thuburbo Majus, Sbeitla, El Djem. But the monuments which are closer to modern Tunisia are those of Islam, and the greatest of them is the mosque of Kairouan. They, no more than Roman, Punic or Byzantine ruins, are the legacy of an earlier Tunisian state. They represent rather the temporary success and independence – sometimes empire – of Muslim rulers. Their passing grandeur has made its contribution to an Arab and Islamic civilization to which Tunisia belongs, in which it can claim pride of place, which enhances its own prestige and importance. The extensive restoration, even rebuilding of such monuments at the present time is evidence of the decline into which they had fallen – and at the same time of their importance in the heritage of the nation.

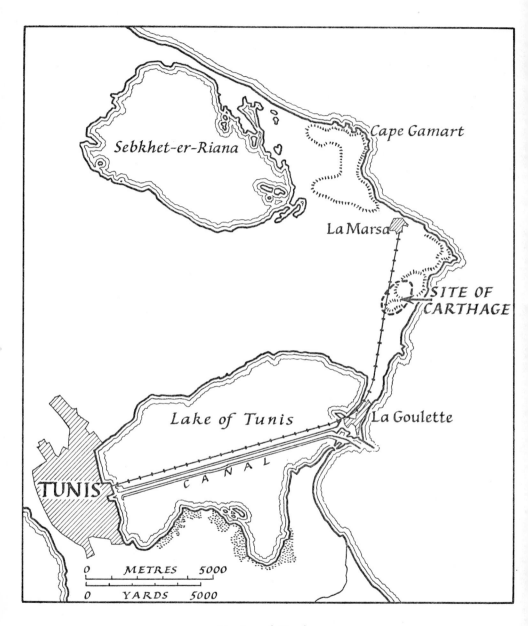

Tunis and Carthage

The French empire left no spectacular monuments, but those it built are for the most part in constant use. They include roads and port installations, post offices and stations. The great cathedrals stand empty, like that of Carthage, or are used as museums, as at Enfida (although mass is still sung in the cathedral of Tunis). French domestic buildings stand out sharply in the countryside, distinguished by their red-tiled roofs from flat-topped white Arab houses. The larger houses often stay unused, inappropriate to a more egalitarian society. But for the most part the remains of the empire form part of the infrastructure of a modern state whose value no Tunisian would underestimate.

The importance of the past to modern Tunisia is not therefore that of continuous history as a nation state, of slow constitutional development or the prolonged defence of established frontiers. For most of its history Tunisia has been part of a larger empire or, in times of weakness, has enjoyed central government only over the more established coastal regions. But there is nothing in the past which Tunisians renounce as alien, and much that they accept with pride. Lacking the exclusiveness of severe Arab nationalists and the intolerance of puritanical Muslims they do not exclude a pre-Arab past from their national heritage as some Middle Eastern Arabs have done. Having liberated themselves by a minimal use of force from imperial rule they neither lack self-confidence nor feel deep bitterness towards a colonial past. The added dimension which the past can bestow on the human personality is evident in the pride with which Tunisians speak of their local monuments; and although such pride may be local rather than national it is never anti-national and only rarely anti-governmental.

There are no tribal or racial divisions in Tunisian society to tear the nation apart. The Arab conquest was grafted on to original Berber stock more completely than in the rest of the Maghreb,[1] and no pockets of Berbers remain as they do in Algeria and Morocco. Few Tunisians speak Berber and none speak only Berber – newsvendors are traditionally Berber, and speak to each other in the language they alone understand. The Arabic which all Tunisians

[1] For notes, see p. 206.

speak makes them part of the Arab world stretching from the Atlantic to the Persian Gulf; although there are strong regional differences from the Arabic of the Middle East, and important differentiations from the language even of Morocco.

French is widely spoken and extensively used as a first language, equal to Arabic. Under the protectorate French was the language of instruction in schools, and Tunisian students went to France to complete their studies. Since independence in 1956, French has been only partially replaced, and that without any over-all pattern being followed. At the lower end of the education scale the battle against illiteracy has been waged to bestow literacy in Arabic, and at the top end of the scale it is still customary for Tunisians to study for degrees in France, or at least to go there for a course of study lasting from three to twelve months. In secondary schools French is still used as a language of instruction – the 2,000 French teachers in Tunisia teach subjects in French as well as the French language – and the range of subjects and scholastic level taught in French rather than Arabic varies. At the time of independence two of the government departments – Justice and Interior – put through a programme of Arabization, with the result that the Directorate of Information now communicates with these two ministries in Arabic, but with Foreign Affairs in French. The question of French versus Arabic is a major preoccupation of sociologists; meanwhile the two co-exist. French has a certain prestige value, as is indicated by the publication of the women's magazine *Faiza* and the now defunct *Carthage*. It has practical importance as a means of acquiring and conveying technical knowledge. Enquiry has shown that a major part of the public use of postal services is in French; at the same time only Arabic is used in the greater part of the villages and countryside.

The homogeneity of the population has increased since independence. French settlers for the most part either left immediately, or did so when their lands were expropriated in 1964. Italians and Greeks accompanied them in their exodus. The important Jewish community diminished progressively as well. Many lower-class Jews went to Israel after the creation of the state, while for others France provided a new home. Precise statistics are not easy to establish;

under the protectorate Tunisian Jews were counted as a separate category of the Tunisian population, but many Jews who had taken French citizenship were registered as French. The Tunisian census makes no distinction according to race and religion. Nevertheless, it is safe to assume that the Jewish population has diminished from some 75,000 to 57,000 – a decline which has to be set against a general population increase of $2\frac{1}{2}$ per cent.

Jewish emigrants have not fled from anti-semitism, which does not exist in Tunisia to any appreciable extent. A minority left as Zionists, or in pursuit of wider opportunities in the new land of Israel. Many more left as Europeans rather than as Jews, finding their traditional occupations less profitable after the departure of the French and the socializing of the economy, or feeling themselves more akin to a French way of life than a Tunisian. Others left through fear – especially in the tense atmosphere of the Arab–Israeli war of June 1967. Before the French protectorate the Jews lived on the edge of Muslim society: their condition improved in the nineteenth century, and the protectorate opened fresh opportunities to them.[2] Fear of a return to the bad old days, accentuated by the loss of Arab lands to the state of Israel, remained after the French went, even though Bourguiba's presidency appeared as a guarantee of security.

Racial and linguistic homogeneity are accompanied by social diversity, even though great individual wealth is rare. Under the protectorate economic enterprise was in French hands, and, since independence, has been controlled by the state. Traditionally certain groups of Tunisians have been noted for their acquisitive drive. Sfax has been the home of private fortunes amassed from olive plantations and the extraction of oil, as well as from general commerce. It provides an example of devout Muslim practice and capitalist enterprise which merits much closer study than has so far been given to it. The island of Jerba has long sent its inhabitants to seek their fortunes as proprietors of grocers' shops – a small but secure foundation on which each might hope to emulate the most successful of their number, like Ben Yedda, the proprietor of a large share of Tunisia's coffee trade.

But the greatest distance in Tunisian society is not so much between the poor and the rich, as between the advanced, sophisticated, moderately well-to-do of the towns and the self-sufficient beduin or the poor and conservative classes of the countryside. Amongst women the gulf is greatest because of the rapid change in the status of women in the more developed parts of the country. Women who work in banks or whose husbands are ministers in Tunis are worlds apart, as their husbands are, from those who scarcely enter into the cash economy at all – who tend their flocks, raise a little wheat, sell a fleece to provide for the most basic cash needs. But they are also separated from those who, though belonging to more modern economic groups, live in traditional society, wearing the veil and separated from men, their social milieu scarcely affected if at all by Bourguiba's reforms and exhortations. Even modernization of economic function carries no guarantee of social progress – in August 1965 Bourguiba expressed his horror at the case of a primary school teacher in Jerba who was to marry a civil servant, and was (to improve her beauty) shut up underground, smeared with clay to give her a fairer complexion and stuffed with spaghetti.

Social and economic diversity is linked to the diversity of the land, which provides Tunisia's principal natural resource and on which four-fifths of the population live. The land is more uniform than that of Morocco and Algeria; the territory is smaller, and there are no high mountains to match those of the Atlas. Such mountains as there are, rising to less than five thousand feet at the highest peak, are situated in the north-east of the country. Oriented from south-west to north-east they attract the rain which is borne on north-westerly winds. The wettest area of Tunisia is thus in the north-west corner, next to the Algerian frontier and the sea. The mountains are covered with trees, including cork oak; the coastal plain and the valley of the Medjerda river (which rises in Algeria) are rich and well-watered – although the use of the land was inefficient and wasteful under the protectorate. This is the region known as the northern Tell, extending as far as Cape Bon. The rainfall follows a roughly regular pattern, diminishing southwards and eastwards. The southern side of the Khroumir mountains, the region of Béja, are thus still well-endowed, though less so than the northern slopes; in the plain of Tunis and Cape Bon, rainfall is adequate, husbanded and directed by irrigation.

The whole of the Tell benefits from the mountains and from proximity to the two coasts, those of the north and the east. South of Cape Bon the influence of the northern coast is left behind; but along the east coast runs the vital region of the Sahel (Arabic for the coast). There is less rain – a yearly average of between 20 and 40 centimetres – but the rainbelt dips slightly down the coast. The climate is softened by the influence of the sea, and the humidity and heavy dews make possible dry farming of olives as far south as Sfax. The Sahel proper runs from Sousse to Mahdia and forms a teeming, crowded, vital, seminal part of Tunisia, the birthplace of Bourguiba and of the Néo-Destour party. Its wealth comes from the land and from the sea. While in most respects Tunisia is sparsely provided with natural riches, it has the advantage of a coastal shelf sloping gradually out to the deep sea – in contrast to the sharper fall which is characteristic of the Mediterranean. The whole of the coast thus provides a harvest of fish, and of sponges off the east coast. The harvest is brought into a string of fishing harbours, as well as to such commercial ports as Sousse and Sfax.

Climate and landscape change abruptly as one travels inland from the Sahel. Average yearly rainfall is the same at Sousse and at Kairouan; but the moderating influence of the sea falls off and the dense thicket of trees and houses gives way to the great windswept plains of central Tunisia. The visual effect of the great Mosque of Kairouan is enhanced thereby – like Chartres it stands aloft like a great beacon, visible from every direction. But instead of the rich wheatfields which provided Péguy with his imagery one sees a harsh land, with sparse plantation, and sand that drifts across the road. With determination it can be brought into greater use. Kairouan itself is now planted with eucalyptus trees which spread outwards along the roads and begin to provide shelter for other trees; pistachios and fruit trees have also begun their defiance of the elements.

The further south the scarcer the rainfall, until one arrives at the edge of the Sahara, whose aridity is relieved by the oases of Gabès,

Gafsa, Tozeur and Nefta. In all this region of central and southern Tunisia life would be easier than it is if rain fell regularly. But the winds which bring the rain to this area come from the north-east, from the Mediterranean. They are not to be depended on, and there are wide variations between maximum and minimum rainfalls. In a bad year crops die and in a good year the water is wasted.

For modern Tunisia diversity in the land – and the recalcitrant nature of the centre and south – provide an immense challenge. In the history of Tunisia there has been a great dividing line drawn across the country separating the north from the south. When government was weak, the north and the Sahel were a prey to the depredations of nomads whenever the lack of rain brought a bad year. In more settled times, the northerners have regarded theirs as the civilized part of the country, while the southerners have been proud of their own toughness and tenacity, born of adversity, in contrast to the easy living of the north.

Within each of the great areas of Tunisia there exists an infinity of smaller divisions. Land use changes rapidly from the wheat of the northern Tell to market gardening – which owes much to Andalusian influence. The rich citrus groves around Nabeul give way rapidly to the more barren uplands of the Cape Bon. Poverty is found side by side with relative wealth – whether on the steep and unexploited slopes of the Khroumir mountains, so close to the fertile coastal plain, or in the Sahel, where real want is hidden in a prosperous and active community.

Cities too have their own intense individuality. Sfax has long been dominated by a small circle of wealthy families – their houses and their gardens surrounding the town testify to their enduring riches and position. Sfaxians have been resistant to outside intrusion to the point that Jerbians, who everywhere else in Tunisia control the retail grocery trade, have never been able to set up shop in Sfax; and they regard the rest of the country with the disdain of those who think of themselves as the real producers of wealth. There is an immense difference between this proud and tight community, sym-bolically surrounded by its ramparts, and the sprawling city of Tunis, hitherto cosmopolitan, still leaning strongly towards Europe, recipient of a population which drifts in steadily from the rest of the country.

Kairouan regards itself as the guardian of the religious heritage of Islamic Maghreb. Its *ulema* are supported by a devout population who rose in demonstration in 1961 against Bourguiba's attacks, as they saw them, on religion. Towns and villages of less renown than Kairouan have their own local loyalty, often based on nothing more than tradition and inbreeding. Bourguiba, in the speech already quoted, inveighed against the practice of not marrying outside the village; in the Sahel there have been fierce disputes between small towns whose separate existence is not immediately obvious to the casual traveller.

In summary the balance of forces in Tunisian society tips in favour of the successful building of a nation, though not decisively. The sources of disunity are not those which have broken other societies. Although the government encounters resistance from Kairouan and elsewhere when modernization seems to infringe religion, it claims to be giving Islam its proper interpretation, and neither attacks religion nor is the exponent of a rival creed. Local rivalries are not the result of tribal diversions; the unsettled future of French as a language of instruction does not affect the ability of all Tunisians to talk to each other. In addition Tunisia is free from external forces which might otherwise attract stormy flood tides of political emotion. The antipathy between Bourguiba and Nasser is matched by the apathy or detachment of Tunisians from Middle Eastern problems, fifteen hundred miles away. Aspirations to Arab leadership of the kind sometimes displayed by Algeria are neither possible nor desirable for a small country with scarce natural resources. Of Tunisia's more immediate neighbours Libya appears an uncultured newly rich country, Algeria turbulent and possibly threatening.

The balance is thus in favour of unity. But the decisive factor thrown into the scale is the political system itself. It has been constructed in such a way as to minimize the divisive forces of society and to strengthen its cohesion. The central animating core of the system has been the leadership of Bourguiba.

2 Carthage

THE EARLY HISTORY of Tunisia merges with legend. Jerba is, according to tradition, the island of the lotus eaters; the Phoenician queen Elissa, sister of the king Pygmalion, became the Dido of Virgil's *Aeneid*. She it was who founded Carthage after escaping from Tyre. She bargained for as much land as an ox-hide would cover, then cut the hide into narrow strips and used them to encircle the hill of Carthage – the byrsa, meaning acropolis in Punic and ox-hide in Greek.

Queen Elissa did not settle in an empty land, but even less is known about the people who already lived there, to whom the Arabs later gave the name Berbers, adapting presumably the Greek word for barbarians. It is thought that they came from the east; they spoke a language which can still be heard in districts from Siwa in Egypt to the Atlantic coast (though much less in Tunisia than in Morocco and Algeria). The language is virtually unwritten and has broken into dialects, without the unifying link of a classical literature. It has survived in place names like Agadir (the fortress), Ifni (the rocky desert), Tsettauen (Tetuan, the springs).[1]

Archaeological evidence for the founding of Carthage is slender, and history is intertwined with legend in classical writings, but scholars now accept the date of 814–813 BC as the origin of this Phoenician colony in the west. It survived until it was destroyed by Rome in the third Punic war of 149–146 BC. After its destruction Punic civilization nonetheless survived in Numidia (now Algeria), where the kingdom founded by the Berber chief Massinissa survived, under Jugurtha,[2] as the inheritor of Punic culture. Customs, traditions and language survived too in Roman Africa.[3]

The foundation of Carthage came during the apogee of Phoenician civilization in the eastern Mediterranean. Inevitably our detailed knowledge of the first millennium BC is slender indeed; yet it is easy to imagine the motives and the drives which made the inhabitants of the Levant coast into colonizers, detaching them from their fellow Canaanites of the interior and sending them to explore and settle the shores of the Mediterranean. Archaeological evidence shows that they first established harbours at sites which have retained their importance ever since – Bizerte, Valetta, Cadiz; while others, now disused, were ideally suited to ships of their scale.

Carthage was such a port, as was Utica further along the coast. The geography of Carthage has changed since Punic times with the silting up of the lakes; then, Sebkret er Riana was open to the sea and the Lake of Tunis also provided shelter for ships. The city of Carthage lay between the two, stretching from La Goulette to La Marsa. The Cothon – ports which served as wet-docks and arsenals – can be assumed to be the small lagoons to the north of Le Kram; the Byrsa on the hill of St Louis. Here, in the temple of Eshmun, the last stand was made in the third Punic war.

Extensive excavation by French scholars has done much to establish the pattern and layout of the city. Nor is it difficult to imagine the strategic strength of a settlement on what was a promontory, with sheltered sea on both sides. The surrounding small hills provided both additional shelter for the ports and suitable sites for rock tombs; the promontory provided land for growing food for the city and there were supplies of fresh water. Further inland it was possible for the wealthy merchants of Carthage to establish villas and gardens on Cape Bon. Of Punic Utica much less is known. Here the configuration of the land has changed even more than at Carthage. The site, which is now six miles from the sea, was once a city and port at the mouth of the Bagradas river (now the Medjerda), with its acropolis on the rising ground of a promontory.

What is the importance to modern Tunisia of a settlement so ancient that the shape of the land has changed since it was founded? Have memories silted like river mouths? To such questions there can be no sure answer. But there can be no doubt of the distinctive contri-

Tunisia and her neighbours

bution which the Phoenicians made to the history of the ancient world. Moreover, once Carthage was founded as an offshoot of eastern Phoenicia it developed its own character, retaining links of language, religion and art with the homeland while becoming a dominant and individual power in the western Mediterranean. It survived by two hundred years the absorption of the Levant into the Greek world after the capture of Tyre by Alexander in 332 BC.

19

Their exploits were astonishing in the history of their time. But they are eclipsed by the inheritance left to the world in the alphabet. In spite of the obscurities surrounding the early history of language, there seems no doubt that the Phoenicians had a decisive part in the invention of the alphabet as a means of written communication. Taken up by the Greeks and other peoples of the Levant, it has provided the basis of all subsequent alphabetic scripts, in the Indo-European and Semitic languages. It is different from pictographs and ideograms in that it bears a purely conventional relationship to sounds and to meaning. It is easily transferable from one language to another, and the computer language of today derives from the script of the Phoenicians.

The Phoenicians depended on military enterprise for their survival and were eventually defeated by the superior resources of Rome. But militarism was the servant of the civilian arts. Although Carthage produced a supreme general in Hannibal, it did not embark on military imperialism for its own sake, and relied for defence on its superiority in ships and on mercenary soldiers. The first battles – and the last in the east – were fought with the Greeks. Unsuccessfully the Carthaginians opposed the establishment of a Greek colony at Marseilles – their failure left the Greeks control (from 600 BC onwards) of the mouth of the Rhône. Throughout the following century the Carthaginians maintained an alliance with the Etruscans against Greek power in the Mediterranean. In 480 BC Phoenician ships fought alongside the Persians and were defeated at Salamis – at the same time as the Carthaginians, acting in concert with the Persians and Phoenicians, failed in an attack on the Greeks and were overcome in the battle of Himera.

The battle did not end the struggle for Sicily, which went on throughout the fifth and fourth centuries. Towards the end of the conflict, at the end of the fourth century BC, Carthage suffered invasion for the first time. Agathocles, tyrant of Syracuse, revolted against the Carthaginians and, escaping from the blockade of his own city, sailed for the African coast. Once ashore (having slipped by the Punic fleet) he encountered no resistance, and marched through the undefended Cape Bon towards Carthage. The Greek historian

Diodorus described the country through which he marched in this way:

> The intervening country through which it was necessary for them to march was divided into gardens and plantations of every kind, since many streams of water were led in small channels and irrigated every part. There were also country houses one after another, constructed in luxurious fashion and covered with stucco, which gave evidence of the wealth of the people who possessed them. The farm buildings were filled with everything that was needful for enjoyment, seeing that the inhabitants in a long period of peace had stored up an abundant variety of products. Part of the land was planted with vines, and part yielded olives and was also planted thickly with other varieties of fruit-bearing trees. On each side herds of cattle and flocks of sheep pastured on the plain, and the neighbouring meadows were filled with grazing horses. In general there was a manifold prosperity in the region, since the leading Carthaginians had laid out there their private estates and with their wealth had beautified them for their enjoyment.[4]

Agathocles failed in his attempt to capture Carthage and, as in the east Alexander had died after his capture of Tyre, the immediate threat to Carthage had disappeared.

But by this time Carthage faced a new rival in the power of Rome. In the perspective of centuries there is still no clear reason why this rivalry between two empires should have escalated into fatal conflict. The power of Rome was on land, and its legionaries marched across the continent of Europe and into Asia, while the Carthaginians exploited the sea routes, seeking resources and trade north to Britain and south round the coasts of Africa. And indeed the first centuries after the rise of Rome were marked by agreements between the two powers, establishing spheres of influence. They fought together in 276 BC to expel Pyrrhus, king of Epirus, from Sicily.

Co-existence did not last. The dramatic episodes of the ensuing conflict have entered into the history learned by every schoolboy brought up on a study of the classical world. The vow of Hannibal to be the implacable enemy of Rome and Cato's incessant incitement to war against Carthage have survived. The evidence necessary to determine more fully the cause of war has long since disappeared and in its default we take it as inevitable that two powers of such magnitude should fight each other.

Once conflict started it left the seeds for renewal. The first Punic war (264–241 BC) ended Carthaginian rule in Sicily and imposed a heavy indemnity. The cost of this indemnity (it is thought) meant that the Carthaginians did not pay their mercenaries and had to fight them instead. Rome claimed Sardinia and a further payment of money in return for neutrality. Confined to the western extremity of the Mediterranean, the Carthaginians established a new Carthage in Spain to serve as a base for the reconquest of the lost empire. From there Hannibal, whose father had gained power as a result of his success in the war with the mercenaries, embarked on the conquest of Rome.

In a stupendous feat of generalship, Hannibal marched with his army and his elephants into Italy, defeated the Romans at Lake Trasimene and at Cannae, and exposed Rome to the greatest danger in its history. Two years after Cannae, in 214 BC, the first reversal occurred as the Romans captured Syracuse. P. Cornelius Scipio Africanus took command in Spain, captured Carthago Nova, and in 204 invaded Africa. The final defeat of this, the greatest of the Punic wars, took place at Zama in 202.

Thereafter for fifty years Carthage was a grievously diminished power. Its fleet was burned and its domain confined to the territorium of north and eastern Tunisia – from the Medjerda valley round to Sousse. Contact was maintained with the existing Punic colonies, but no others could be founded. Carthage could undertake no war without Roman consent, and was contained on its western borders by Massinissa, the ally of Rome, established as king of Numidia in reward for his help in the war.

It was this which gave Rome the pretext for the last and final war. When Carthage attacked Massinissa in order to oppose his depredations of Carthaginian territory, Rome declared war in 149 BC, and three years later Carthage was destroyed, burned and razed to the ground.

Much that is known about the Phoenicians comes from excava-
tions at Carthage, since the constant building and rebuilding of
towns along the Levant coast has left little opportunity for academic
digging. Later history is known from the accounts of Greek and
Roman historians. From what was written at the time, it is clear that
the Phoenicians established a unique empire, tying together widely
disseminated colonies and controlling their trade, while leaving them
autonomy. The centre of the confederacy in the west was Carthage,
which extended its rule over the fertile lands of present-day Tunisia.
It governed the Berbers within its dominion, collected taxes and recruited soldiers for the army. But even cities like Utica and Hadrumetum (Sousse) retained their autonomy, in spite of being dependent on Carthage for their security.

A colony was established in Sardinia in the sixth century BC, and,
after the first Punic war, in Spain, centred on Carthago Nova. Over
these colonies Carthage ruled directly. In Sardinia colonists were
brought from Africa and a province established in the plains to the
south and west, while at the same time the mineral resources of lead
and silver were developed. The purpose of the colony was no doubt
to serve as a barrier to the Greeks. Over the other colonies control
was indirect – no fixed garrisons were maintained, nor was there any
maritime equivalent of the Roman army. Immensely strong in
commerce, the empire had thus no defence in depth against military
attack.

Often the most direct link between ourselves and an ancient
civilization is to be found in its art and artifacts. But the remains of
Punic civilization do not readily appeal to a modern sense of beauty;
they lack both stark simplicity of form and refinement of detail.
Inevitably they carry a certain fascination – together with the frustra-
tion which accompanies our lack of knowledge. Amongst the most
distinctive Punic creations are a series of masks – female, smiling
or impassive masks, other which are male, grinning and grotesque.
An outstanding authority, P. Cintas, has distinguished four clearly
distinct types of mask, and we know that they were placed in tombs,
presumably to safeguard the dead. Any other purpose they served,
and the meaning of the different types is unknown.

Greece and Egypt had a strong influence on Phoenician art – and the styles and traditions of the east were carried to Carthage. So too were ready-made pottery, and (presumably) moulds for the making of figurines. As elsewhere religious practice was responsible for a large part of artistic output, and the stelae associated with temples have survived in numbers. Greek influence is obvious here too; but the distinctive symbolism of Punic religion helps to ensure that a certain rude individual style shows through. The engravings on the stelae are of the god Tanit, symbolized representations of her, or an even more conventionalized 'sign of Tanit'. They also show motifs of plants and animals, fishes, birds and frogs. Moreover the survival of Punic religion meant that such stelae continued to be made under the Romans. Amongst the most highly developed are Ghorfa stelae (now in the Bardo museum) which date from the second century AD.

The stelae testify to the pervasiveness of religion in the world of Carthage; yet here too our knowledge is slender. It scarcely extends beyond the names of the dominant gods and the fact that sacrifice was at the centre of religious practice. Tanit, Pene Baal and Baal Hammon were identified by the Greeks and Romans as Hera/Juno and Kronos/Saturn, and they obviously predominated over the local deities which thrived in the autonomy of the Punic world. These gods demanded sacrifices, and the best was given them – so that excavation reveals a multitude of urns containing the bones of children. Animals and birds were also acceptable to the gods; prisoners were sacrificed to them, whether in thanks or expiation.

As in other civilizations the care taken over the dead has ensured the survival of minor artifacts buried in tombs. So we have examples of jewelry and amulets, scarabs and razors. For the archaeologist they are immensely evocative, and clearly show links with the eastern Mediterranean – with Egypt as well as with Phoenicia.

The absence of literary sources and of monuments limits our knowledge of the Carthaginian world, and the artifacts that remain lack the beauty that has survived from other civilizations. The enduring appeal of the Carthaginians is in their enterprise and adventure, the daring and persistence of their exploration and their skill in establishing a commercial empire of autonomous cities. Trade was developed as part of a deliberate policy, and governed from Carthage. Markets were opened by force and a monopoly of trade reserved to Carthaginian or Phoenician colonies where this was possible; elsewhere a division of trade was arranged by treaty. Navigation was protected and piracy put down. All round the Mediterranean ports were established, with a day's sailing between each.

The prosperity of the Phoenician world was based above all on trade in precious metals; Carthage became the centre in the west for the exploration of the metal routes. Silver was found in Spain, so was tin – and of this there were further supplies in Britain. Gold came from Africa. These were metals which had little value in the west, but could be traded for a far higher price in the east. Because of the importance of metal – and also no doubt because of the commercial resourcefulness of the Phoenicians – voyages of exploration were undertaken far beyond the comparatively safe and known waters of the Mediterranean. In the fifth century Himilco sailed up the Atlantic coast of Europe to the British Isles and visited Ireland. Hanno explored the Atlantic coast of Africa, and his account of his journey, in a Greek version, has survived to us.[5] The Phoenicians may have sailed to the Canaries, the Azores and Madeira; and they travelled overland across the Sahara in search of gold.

The civilization which was built on this material basis did not immediately disappear under the Romans. Their occupation (in the second century AD) was at first on a limited scale; for a long time it left the practice of religion intact, and the use of language undisturbed.

Nonetheless the victory of Rome opened a new era in the region which was to become Tunisia. It was now brought into close and direct contact with Europe for some five centuries. It was at the southern border of a dominion that came to stretch northwards to Hadrian's Wall and eastwards to the borders of Persia. Within that empire it had a place of major importance, supplying Rome with grain and foodstuffs, making a vital contribution to the development of the Latin language and of Christian theology.

That it should do so was the result in part of the tranquillity which the empire brought – in contrast to many of the other outlying provinces. Then, as now, north-west Africa was protected by the seas and surrounding deserts in a way in which the German frontier of the Roman empire was not. This was particularly true of the eastern part of the territory – proconsular Africa, embracing Tunisia and the coastal strip of Tripolitania. Defence forces were small in number – some 13,000 men in Tripolitania, Tunisia and eastern Algeria, at a maximum. The security of the territory is evident in the remains of towns throughout Tunisia, testimony to a settled life in the interior as well as in the more easily defensible coastal area. At the height of the empire only a frontier force was necessary to safeguard Africa along the Sahara.

Security from attack and internal safety were accompanied by insulation from the central power of Rome and from its quarrels. North Africa was neither on the route to other parts of the empire nor the starting point for revolt. In the twentieth century, North Africa has twice changed the politics of Europe – when Franco's army invaded Spain and when the Algerian army brought de Gaulle to power in France. Only once in the history of the empire did an African governor – Gordian – make a bid for supreme power in Rome (in 238 AD). He did so reluctantly, urged on by a discontented bourgeoisie, and he was unsuccessful.

The pattern which characterized the relations of the eastern provinces with Rome was thus not repeated in the west. The African proconsul had only limited forces at his command, and his authority was balanced by that of the Emperor's representative and of the army commander. He held office for a year at a time. The exercise of authority in Africa opened the way to higher office in the empire rather than inspiring revolt.

The mosaics which survive in Tunisia – which make the Bardo museum so outstanding, and the museum of every Tunisian town worth a visit – provide a vivid portrayal of life under the empire. They show the variety of agriculture, which included wheat growing, the cultivation of olives, mixed farming. Fishing was a major source of food, and commerce and shipping flourished. As the Mediterranean was made secure by Roman sea power, boats plied their way ceaselessly between African ports – Carthage, Hadrume-

26

tum (Sousse), Leptis – and Ostia. Savage wild life was more abundant than now, and provided sport and food when hunted.

As significant as the precise evidence which the mosaics provide of particular occupations is the grace and delicacy with which they are composed. One of the most lastingly beautiful of them is a bird in a cage. These are works of a settled and serene civilization, where men had time to enjoy life and to portray grace and beauty.

Not that the life of Africa, any more than the rest of the Roman empire, was one of quiet and civilized pursuits. One of the greatest monuments remaining in Tunisia is the colosseum of El Djem, standing like a mountain as one drives along the straight road from Sousse to Sfax. It was the scene of those amusements which allayed the boredom of rich men and released the frustrations of the poor – as gladiators fought with each other or men struggled with wild beasts. We know from the writings of Tertullian that the Romans eventually took vigorous action against the continuance of infant sacrifice practised by the Carthaginians: they were less sensitive to the lives of the showmen of gladiatorial combats.

While Carthaginian monuments have almost entirely disappeared, Roman building shows the same durability in Tunisia as elsewhere. The great amphitheatre of El Djem would be almost intact today had not a Bey of Tunis breached its walls to quell insurgents who had made it their fort. The aqueduct which the Romans built to bring water from Zaghouan to Tunis was thought worth reconstructing for use in the nineteenth century.

The survival of Roman monuments makes it easy to reconstruct the shape of towns. Whether a town was built on open ground or (as was most often the case) on the site of a Punic settlement, it had the same essential features. The central square – the forum – was surrounded by the main public buildings: city hall, law court and commercial centre. Nearby were the temples to the three supreme gods of the Roman religion. If possible, these were placed on an elevation in the ground. If none were there a platform was constructed, as can be seen at Thuburbo Majus.

At Dougga the Romans, building on the site of a Numidian town (of which a mausoleum still remains), brought unusual diver sity into the arrangement of the buildings. The town is built on the side of a steep hill with a magnificent view over the Khalled river and the main road from Carthage to Theveste which ran along it. The temple was arranged so that its façade faced over the valley instead of towards the forum, and was thus visible to travellers on their journey through the valley. The rest of the town followed the same theme. The austere alignment of streets to be found in nearly all Roman towns was abandoned to meet the demands of a hillside; the houses were kept at a lower level and the crest of the hill was surmounted by a rising series of religious and public buildings, with the temple to Jupiter and a theatre at the top.[6]

Such towns are testimony above all to the wealth and prosperity of Roman Africa from the first to the third century AD. During this period population increased steadily, rising to six and a half and eight million in the province as a whole – the density in Tunisia being perhaps rather less than at the present time. At the beginning of the Roman occupation the wealth of the province came almost entirely from grain. The imperial government made an imperial levy on grain from the African provinces, and soon after the conquest Africa provided Rome with two-thirds of its supply, the rest coming from Egypt. The short haul from North Africa was an obvious economy in supplying the capital. Even when the levy was paid, the extension of cultivated estates in Mauretania and Numidia left an increasing amount of wealth in the hands of Roman settlers – ill-distributed as it was.

As the province developed a more diversified agriculture re-appeared, and the ravages of conquest were made good. With imperial encouragement land was recovered and made suitable for grain cultivation. Then at the end of the first century settlers from North Africa, acting as a pressure group in Roman politics, brought an end to the privileges enjoyed hitherto by Italy in the production of olives. The result was that an immense olive oil industry grew up, with important ancillary industries surrounding it. Its greatest concentration was then in the same area as it is now – around Thysdrus, Sufetula (Sbeitla) and in the Ousseltia valley. In Tunisia the growth of cereals as a single crop became very exceptional, even in areas especially suited to it such as that round Béja and the upper Medjerda valley.

The wealth coming from olive oil paid for the colosseum of El Djem. For oil was not only a principal source of food; it provided fuel for lamps and the base for toilet preparations. The pressing of the olives and the export of oil were major industries in themselves; the demand for receptacles led to the growth of a pottery industry, and the fact that oil was available in plenty for lighting meant that lamps of infinitely varied design were produced in thousands. Africa thus became an exporter of pottery. It also exported textiles, especially those dyed with Phoenician purple from Jerba and Chullu (Collo, on the Constantine coast). It is probable, says Charles-Picard, that in the third century Africa exported as much in manufactured goods as it imported – the imports consisting primarily of metal goods.

Export and import trade led to the development of ports. Of those which the Phoenicians had built some were developed – for instance, Carthage and Hadrumetum. Others served primarily as fishing ports. Clupea (Kelibia) was important, so was the nearby Missua (Sidi Daoud) from which construction material (*calcaire coquillier*) was sent to Carthage. The greatest of the ports which the Romans reconstructed lies outside modern Tunisia – at Leptis Magna, in Libya. The wadi which had formed the Punic port was given a new channel to prevent it silting up, and a massive mole with portside warehouses was constructed.

The province would not have been Roman had not good roads ensured its communication – roads which were seldom paved, but constructed rather with a hard surface of gravel. They linked Carthage with the important fortress towns of Theveste, Timgad and Lambaesis (all of them in modern Algeria). But roads were built and used for commerce and travel as well, linking the important towns and the ports of Tunisia and joining that part of the province westwards to the Atlantic coast and eastwards to Egypt.

Wealth and commerce have always been associated with the development of towns, and nowhere was this more so than in Africa where security was greatest. The growth of towns and cities in turn meant the extension of the domain of Roman law and the growth of civic liberty. The social pyramid of the Roman empire was very steep, but there were no ethnic barriers in the African province, and under the empire anyone who was free (in the sense of not being a slave) could become a full member of a Roman town. Saint Augustine himself was the son of a farmer who sacrificed much for his education in order to enable him to climb the social scale. The concentration of cities and towns in eastern Africa made Roman citizen rights that much easier to achieve, even though the social pyramid remained so steep.

In the countryside there were immense gaps between the wealthy landowners and the rural poor. Nonetheless a high proportion of those living in the province enjoyed the benefits of Roman urban civilization. Above all they came under the fair disposition of the Roman law, created as it was over the centuries of the republic and the empire. Roman law, it has been said, 'displays practical common sense at its highest and best, embodied in thought and language of extreme clarity and sharpness.'[7] It framed generalizations to meet the problems which arose in civilized society, rather than drawing on principles conceived in a theocratic or ideological mould; and no legal generalizations have achieved wider or more long-lasting acceptance than those of Rome.

Roman law did not at first guarantee the rights or the safety of minority groups – especially that most disruptive minority, the Christians. Yet it was within the ordered society of Rome that North Africans made their own decisive contribution to Latin civilization. Tertullian, who can be regarded as the creator of Latin Christian literature, was born in Carthage in AD 150. In defence of the Church (and later in defence of the Donatist sect) he became a great propagandist. Educated in Latin and Greek, he first wrote in Greek, but then increasingly in Latin, developing a style of his own, drawing on a popular tradition rather than the oratorical style of Cicero and giving it all the vigour of his African background. He was followed by Cyprian, who from 249 was Bishop of Carthage during a decade of plague and persecution; until he succumbed to the Valerian persecution, to be canonized by the Church.

Both Tertullian and Cyprian were surpassed by Augustine,

Bishop of Hippo, who was born across the present Algerian frontier at Thagaste – Souk Ahras – in 354. He grew up in Carthage and Italy before returning to Hippo, in the diocese of Carthage, and dividing his time between there and Carthage for the rest of his life.[8]

He was a sensitive yet combative individual living in a period of turbulence; at once deeply self-aware and inward-looking and constantly dependent on the company of others. His stay in Italy and his own studies made him a member of the community of learning of the Roman empire; but he retained the drive and the fire of his origins. His teaching was to an audience of his fellow countrymen; his writings met the arguments of his contemporaries on their own ground. Constantly engaged in verbal combat, he directed his arguments towards a specific audience, whether it was to the members of his own church in North Africa, or to the readers of Plotinus and Porphyry; yet he created a literature of enduring value.

He was brought up in Catholicism at a time when it had been newly imposed on pagan culture, and then attracted to the religion of the Manichees – the followers of Mani, an eastern prophet, executed in Mesopotamia in AD 276, who claimed a direct revelation from God. The Manichees saw the world as divided between the forces of light and the forces of evil; good being a passive sphere which could at best be maintained intact against the onslaught of evil.

Manicheeism was powerful doctrine; its followers established communities from China to the Atlantic. But Augustine's attachment to it did not last. At the age of thirty-two he was appointed to a chair in Milan, and it was there that he was converted to Catholicism in a creative, innovating form such as he had not known before. His conversion lacked much of the sensation later attributed to it: his earlier life had not been dissolute, and his conversion consisted of a further, though deeply affective stage in his development rather than a total break with the past. But this did not lessen the degree of his commitment to the doctrines of the Catholics, which from that time he did as much to create as to defend.

His defence of Catholicism was not solely or even mainly against other philosophers. When he returned to Carthage in 388 the Church in Africa was divided between Catholics and Donatists – a rift which had its origins in the reaction of the clergy to persecution by the imperial authorities. In 303 bishops and priests were faced with an edict requiring scriptures to be surrendered and churches dismantled. They chose variously between different degrees of resistance and suffering; some refused and were taken to prison, some handed over heretical texts pretending that they were scriptures. The enduring human problem of whether to offer integral resistance or to bend before the storm divided the Church, as it has divided societies before and since. The Donatists stood against all compromise, taking their name from their claimant to the see of Carthage.

The problem did not remain within the confines of the Church in Africa. It was brought before Constantine, thus opening up the whole problem of the relationship of a Christian emperor to the Church. As late as 411, after the sack of Rome, Augustine himself took the leading part in challenging the Donatists at the conference of Carthage, after which the laws against them were strictly enforced.

In the intervening years official support for the Catholic Church had given the dispute more of the character of a conflict between rich and poor. The issue was one of almost universal human and political importance – the Donatists made a claim to purity and exclusiveness, while the Catholics imposed less rigorous demands on the members of the Church and aimed, therefore, at wider comprehension. But the effect of persecution was that Donatist bishops were removed from the cities, where the wealthier townspeople supported the Catholics, while the poor in the countryside flocked to the Donatist priests. They had the support, too, of wilder bands of men, the Circumcellions – bands of 'holy' men who moved around the countryside celebrating the lives of martyrs at their shrines, men whose counterparts in the Islamic faith survived in North Africa into modern times, and fanatics who resorted readily to maiming and murder. Augustine, whose diocese was initially dominated by Donatists, himself escaped ambush by the Circumcellions.

The environment in which Augustine grew up was thus very particular. Yet the Carthage of his day was the second city of the Roman empire, and as the defences of that empire crumbled before the Picts and Scots in the north and the German tribes in the east, the African province grew in importance. The controversies of Africa thrived in an atmosphere of provincialism, where the participants were known to each other and feelings could run with all the heat of an enclosed world – but their repercussions extended to the government of the empire itself.

The contribution of Augustine was even more universal. The output of his teaching and writing was prodigious, and from the sum total of it the *Confessions* and the *City of God* have so far entered into a Christian and European heritage that one has to be reminded of the immediate surroundings which evoked their writing.

The *Confessions* were written from the standpoint of a mature man who had passed through Manicheeism and neo-Platonism to become a Christian bishop, who had experienced a peculiarly intense relationship with his mother and lived through her sudden death. They form an autobiography which explores feelings and thought with deep sensitivity, and which describe a man as the product of his past – while describing that past in terms defined by the present.

The *City of God* was written at the end of Augustine's life, provoked by the arrival in Carthage of a Roman aristocracy fleeing the capital after its sack by Alaric, intruding a neo-paganism into the small but Catholic world of Augustine's Africa. In response to this challenge Augustine linked the classical world to that of medieval Christian Europe. The arguments and the standards he was called on to meet were those of revered and respected Roman and Greek authors; in doing so he expounded the idea of a heavenly city whose citizens were temporary travellers in the earthly world, bringing with them, cultivating and propagating the habits and ideals of the city of God. 'So the *City of God*, far from being a book about flight from the world, is a book whose recurrent theme is "our business within this common mortal life"; it is a book about being other-worldly in the world.'[9]

Augustine died as the Roman empire in Africa collapsed. For so long secure behind its frontiers of sea and desert, the empire was defenceless once the straits of Gibraltar were crossed. In 429 Genseric, king of the Vandals, led such an attack, quickly overrunning

33

Mauretania and Numidia, and laying waste Roman and Catholic civilization alike. In 435 he made a treaty with Rome; but four years later extended his kingdom into Tunisia and established the seat of his government in Carthage.

The Vandals proved incapable of establishing their own civilization in Africa. They sought to impose their religion by force, and their rule was at first characterized by persistent violence, which only gave way to tolerance as their society became more effete. They were Arians – followers of the Alexandrian priest Arius, who denied the divinity of Christ on the grounds that the Godhead, being unique, could not be shared or communicated. Their doctrines had been condemned by the Council of Nicaea in 325, but this did not end belief in them (any more than it prevented their revival in the eighteenth century by Samuel Clarke, the rector of St James's, Westminster).

The destructiveness of the Vandals has no doubt been exaggerated, and is certainly not sufficiently distinctive to justify the use of their name as a descriptive term for iconoclasm and hooliganism. But their persecution had all the harshness of religious intolerance added to the conflict between conquerors and subjects. It was described at the time by the Catholic bishop of Vita in Tunisia, Victor, whose *Historia persecutionis Africanae provinciae* described the 'savagery, cruelty and terror' of his new rulers and said:

> One may coddle them with kindness, woo them with assiduous service, all they think of is their envy of the Romans. Their design is obvious, all the time they are trying to besmirch the glory and honour of the Roman name. Their desire is that no Romans shall survive. If they spare their subjects in one or another case, it is to exploit them as slaves. For they have never had any affection for Romans, even as individuals.[10]

The Vandals ruled in North Africa for a century, until their dominion was replaced by an equally brief period of Byzantine rule, from 534 until the beginning of the Arab invasions in the middle of the seventh century. The reconquest of North Africa was the work of the Byzantine general Belisarius, under the command of Emperor Justinian, whose greatest monument is St Sophia in Istanbul.

The new Roman empire, established in Constantinople, showed greater resilience in the face of external attack than did Rome itself – or at least it survived as long as the Dardanelles gave Constantinople a natural defence against invasion. But north-west Africa was far from the centre of the empire, and although Belisarius had succeeded in defeating the Vandals, neither he nor his successors could establish a continuing authority over the Berber tribes, who could always find refuge in the steppe and the mountains.

Once the fabric of Roman rule had been torn, it was thus not easily mended. Byzantine rule was weakened by theological dispute, and by distance from the centre. It remained precarious in the face of Berber revolt, Meanwhile Roman buildings remained, or were slowly broken down as their stones were used for humbler shelters; the roads continued to be used into the Middle Ages. Much of the way of life of the Sahel and Jerba remained too – in large part it ante-dated Roman rule.

In a more general sense the Roman experience had been of vital relevance to the history of what is now Tunisia. The conflicts and political issues of Roman Africa were of provincial importance; but the attachment of North Africa to a wider European culture enabled it to make a distinctive contribution, especially in the work of St Augustine, to the intellectual inheritance of the western world.

3 Muslim rule and Hilalian invasion

IN THE YEAR 622 Muhammad left Mecca for Medina. His emigration (Hejira, from the Arabic) has since been taken as the start of the Muslim calendar, for at this point Muhammad ceased to be regarded as a single if unusual individual and was recognized as the chief magistrate of the Medinese community. In 630 the Muslims returned and conquered Mecca. Two years later, on 8 June 632, Muhammad died. By that time he had established a new religion, endowed with its own sacred book which embodied (for believers) the word of God transmitted through the Prophet. It replaced pagan religion with belief in a single God and introduced ethical codes which called for a higher level of conduct than those it replaced. The Koran and the traditions (Hadith) of the Prophet's life were developed into intricate rules governing every aspect of normal life, upheld by five central pillars – declaration of belief in God, alms, fasting, prayer and pilgrimage.

At the time of Muhammad's death the Muslims were already organized into a strong political and religious community. In the next fifty years their faith, their political and social organization and their ability for war carved out an Islamic empire from the Atlantic to the Indus. It was an unstable empire not only because of its extent, but because, while the authority of Muhammad was never questioned, the succession to him and the meaning of his teaching were a permanent matter of dispute.

Nonetheless the empire of Islam formed a distinctive civilization neighbouring that of Christian Europe, often concerned with similar problems of moral and political authority. The two civilizations were for long centuries in conflict, though each drew something from a common Greek heritage. As the conflict subsided the penetration of trade and commerce deepened, to be followed at last by mutual understanding.

Across northern Africa Arab armies, small in number, ranged from Egypt into Cyrenaica and Fezzan, then westwards to Tripoli. They met little resistance from Byzantine rulers. In 647 the first Arab raid in pursuit of booty was made into Tunisia. The Byzantine patriarch Gregory rallied a Berber army at Sbeitla, but was easily defeated. The Arab leader Ibn Sa'd retired with the loot which had formed the object of the raid. The next major incursion did not occur until after the establishment of the Umayyad dynasty at Damascus, when it was led by Mu'awiya ibn Hudaij. Five years later, in 670, came a third expedition, this time with the object of establishing permanent Arab rule in Tunisia. It was led by Uqba ibn Nafi, and he it was who established a *place d'armes* – in Arabic *Qairawan*, or in the more familiar French transliteration, *Kairouan* – on the plain of Tunisia, inland from Sousse.

For the second time Tunisia had thus become part of a civilization with its centre and starting point in the east – as the Phoenicians had come by sea to Carthage, so now the Arabs came by land and established their citadel in the desert, while the Byzantines still controlled the ports. But the distinctive characteristics of the Arab west (the Maghreb) – and even of the land which eventually became Tunisia – constantly reasserted themselves. Berber resistance and revolt lasted long after the first Arab victories; Berber and Arab dynasties established in the Maghreb were independent of the Arab east; and in the tenth century a ruler of what is now Tunisia struck eastwards to establish a new dynasty which ruled Egypt for two centuries from 969. From North Africa these dynasties carried out the conquest of half of Spain, to be followed by the interpenetration of the two civilizations of the western Mediterranean. From then until the present century there was no period in which some part of one side of the Gibraltar straits was not ruled from the other.

From 670 until the end of the next century Kairouan remained a garrison city like Kufa and Basra in Iraq, or Fustat in Egypt – 'the

Gibraltars and Singapores of the early Arab empire'.[1] It was a centre of Arab rule in Berber territory, the starting point of expeditions, the stronghold to be vanquished in time of revolt. The Arabs were as yet too few in numbers to establish effective government over the Berber tribes. They could undertake extensive raids, but were vulnerable to attack. Uqba himself is supposed to have led an expedition across north-west Africa to the Atlantic coast where, legend has it, he asked God to witness that the sea prevented him going further. But he was over-extended. Berber and Byzantine resistance under the leadership of the obscure leader Kusaila brought the defeat of his forces and his own death at Tahoudha. His burial place – Sidi Uqba – became a shrine of pilgrimage. Meanwhile Kusaila had entered Kairouan, only to suffer a reversal of fortune and the same fate as Sidi Uqba three years later, in 686.

Berber resistance then passed to a yet more romantic (though, in default of documents and inscriptions, no less obscure) figure – Kahina, or the 'prophetess'. Her name is unknown; according to Ibn Khaldun she professed Judaism, and she ruled the Maghreb like some North African Boadicea for five years. But the Arabs grew steadily stronger, and by this time they had defeated their other foe, the Byzantines. Hassan ibn al-Nu'man al-Ghassani conquered Carthage in 695 and, recovering from defeat at the hands of Kahina, recaptured the city in 698. Having done so he built a new port – Tunis – at the end of the small gulf, protected from raids from the sea. The sea-power of Byzantium in the western Mediterranean was now broken, and the Arabs faced a single enemy, the Berbers, on land. Against Kahina they were victorious, in a battle which probably took place near Tabarka. She was slain and her head sent in triumph to the Caliph. Hassan set about establishing a settled system of government, exacting regular taxes and extending his rule westwards. He knocked down Sidi Uqba's mosque in Kairouan and built another, bringing marble pillars from Carthage to strengthen and embellish his work.

But insurrection continued, and, linked to other movements in the Islamic world, came to assume a religious and ideological form. In the Arab east the succession to the headship of the Islamic community – the Caliphate – divided Muslims amongst themselves only twenty-five years after Muhammad's death. The majority came to be known as Sunnis, believing in the election of the Caliph from the tribe of the Prophet; while others, followers of Muhammad's son-in-law Ali, were known as Shi'ites ('partisans' of Ali). At a key point in the contest for leadership – following the battle of Siffin in 657 – Ali had allowed his claim to be submitted to arbitration. Thereupon the more extreme of his followers revolted against him and were bloodily suppressed. They came to be known as Kharijites – 'those who go out'.

The Kharijites had their own solution to the problem of the Caliphate. They believed that anyone could be Caliph, even a black slave, provided that he was of sufficient merit; and the community were the judge of merit, both in choosing a Caliph and in destituting him. They were rigorous and puritanical, requiring works as well as faith as a means to salvation – and in the environment in which they lived works most frequently meant war and violence. Ali him-self was murdered by a Kharijite called Ibn Muljam.

With the defeat of Ali and the establishment of the Umayyad dynasty in Damascus the Kharijites survived in Iraq and spread in groups throughout the Arab world, particularly to North Africa. They professed Islam in a version which legitimized violence and bred anarchy. Egalitarian, puritanical, claiming direct divine inspira-tion, they represented an extreme version of the non-conformity which characterizes most rigorous religions, while at the same time mobilizing – it may be assumed – the discontent of the poor and the tribal feelings of the Berbers. It is tempting to see them, as some writers have done, as the inheritors of the more extreme wing of Donatism, and to imagine the Berbers who now resisted Arab government as being the descendants of the Circumcellions.

Against the Kharijite rebellion it became impossible to establish ordered government for any long period. In 756 Kharijites invaded and sacked Kairouan, so that the citizens had to take refuge outside the town. Meanwhile in the east the Abbasid house had replaced the Umayyads as leaders of the Islamic community. An Abbasid governor of Egypt, Ibn Ash'ath, took personal command of an expedition to vanquish the Kharijites and free Kairouan. After a series of campaigns his armies were successful and Kharijite power was destroyed in Tunisia – but survived to form an independent kingdom at Tahert in the west. In Tunisia the remnants of insurrection were crushed by Yazid ibn Hatim, and this formed the prelude to the establishment of a new dynasty under the nominal suzerainty of the Abbasid caliphate. Its first ruler was an Arab regional governor, Ibrahim ibn Aghlab. He took the title of Amir and was in practice independent of Egypt.

Aghlabid rule lasted undisturbed throughout the ninth century. It extended somewhat beyond the boundaries of present-day Tunisia and included the greater part of Roman Africa (which passed into Arabic as 'Ifriqiya'). But effective government was strongest and most continuous in the settled areas of the east coast of Tunisia, and in the south, where Yazid ibn Hatim had quelled the Kharijites. The population was still mixed and divided. The Arabs had not yet fused with the Berbers. The latter had accepted Islam, but this was far from adequate to win them the esteem of the Arabs; they remained a conquered people. Christian communities remained – the Kairouan museum includes Christian inscriptions, the Greek lettering of which shows Arabic influence. There were important groups of Jews in the towns, many of them doctors.

Kairouan was the capital of the Aghlabid amirate. At this time the city enjoyed its period of greatest splendour. The great mosque was once again rebuilt. It was made twice as big, and constructed in accordance with the architectural pattern established in the Arab east, as it can be seen today. With its four hundred and fourteen columns dividing the single great prayer hall into seventeen naves it was and is an impressive and moving structure. Outside is a wide and spacious court, on the other side the great minaret, built in three stages. Then, as now, it dominated the surrounding plain, rising above the low buildings of the town and the smaller minarets of innumerable other mosques, a single tall edifice in a harsh landscape. Other mosques were built at Kairouan, including the Mosque of the three doors; so was the Zitouna mosque at Tunis, and others at Sousse and Sfax.

Monastir too enjoyed a golden age under the Aghlabids. For this was a period of great theological discussion and intense devotion. The *ribat* of Monastir was the first to be founded in the Arab west, and it has been suggested that the name of the town derives from the appellation given by Latin-speaking Berbers to the Arab *ribat* or monastery. A century after its foundation the Traditions of the Prophet were quoted to show that it was blessed land, and that those buried there would go to paradise. The *ribat* itself was rebuilt by the Aghlabids, who also constructed another along the coast at Sousse. The *ribats* were the centres of an austere and ascetic religious life; they were also military installations, defensive fortresses and – in the case of the Sousse – the point of departure for military expeditions.

Peace in Tunisia was accompanied by expansion across the Mediterranean. The dynasty had been founded after a period of civil strife which had left a fund of military restlessness as its legacy. Across the sea in Sicily was a tempting prize, and in 827 an expedition landed on the island. Conquest was pursued over a period of decades in a desultory manner. Neither Byzantine resistance nor rival expeditions from Venice inflicted any serious reverse on the Muslim invaders, and by the beginning of the tenth century the conquest was complete.

The occupation of Sicily was surpassed by the achievements of the dynasty in its own society. Kairouan became not only the settled and civilized capital of the amirate, but one of the centres of devotion and learning of the Islamic world. Theological issues were ardently debated, as they were to be in medieval Europe. At the heart of the debate between the ascetics and devout men of Kairouan were questions about the origin of the Koran – whether, being the word of God, it had always existed throughout eternity, or whether (as the Mutazilites argued) it had been created.

Legal debates were joined to theological. It was at this time that the Malikite code of law was established in Tunisia, later to spread throughout North Africa. A group of scholars at Kairouan, of whom the most important was Suhnun, interpreted the Malikite law, distinguished it from the less austere doctrines of Hanafism, and ensured its predominance. But for all the intensity of Islamic devotion and theological argument Kairouan remained a centre of Jewish learning as well. The physician to the Aghlabid amir Ziyadat Allah II was a Jew named Ishaq ibn Imran, who was a renowned teacher of medicine, as was his pupil Ishaq ibn Sulaiman. For Jewish culture as for Islam, ninth-century Kairouan was a golden period.

But not all was learning and austere theology, neither of which was to the taste of the Aghlabid rulers. They built for themselves great palaces outside Kairouan – Kasr al-Kadim which was constructed to the south-east at the beginning of the dynasty and the more important and imposing al-Raqqada, to the south-west, built by Ibrahim ibn Ahmad in 876–7. The palace of al-Raqqada was surrounded by a thriving town, with bazaars, baths, parks and gardens – the whole enclosed by an immense wall. Great efforts were made to control and conserve the supply of water. (In times of heavy rainfall the wadis round Kairouan overflow and floods come to the wall of the town; as the rainfall ends the land dries rapidly and the roads disappear under drifts of driving sand.) Ziyadat Allah I and Ibrahim constructed waterworks, of which the most important were restored centuries later by French engineers. As a result an immense reservoir – *le bassin des Aghlabites* – still holds its cool and limpid water (now half surrounded by eucalyptus trees, planted since independence), ingeniously designed to provide filtration between the two parts of the reservoir and having in the centre a restored remnant of what was once an octagonal tower and pavilion.

The museum of Kairouan retains the memorials of the dual aspect of Aghlabid society. A collection of marble memorials carved with Kufic inscriptions testifies to the austerity and puritanism of men whose religion permitted no other decoration – and who could not for all that destroy the creative spirit of those who made Kufic writing a thing of beauty in itself. The ceramics which have been excavated from al-Raqqada, more exotically decorated, are the most evocative reminder of a life of pleasure and enjoyment, of gardens and baths to alleviate the arid heat of the plain, trees to give shade from the sun and shelter from the wind, of feasting and dancing, drunkenness and debauchery.

But the achievements of the Aghlabid dynasty were insufficient to ensure its perpetuation, or a peaceful succession. There was little continuity in the style of the Aghlabid rulers, so that qualities of statesmanship alternated with drunkenness and cruelty (sometimes in the same ruler). Great as are the physical constructions of the period they were no substitute for constructive government – for a satisfactory tax system, or economic development. At the beginning of the tenth century the Aghlabid dynasty collapsed before the on-slaught of Shi'ism, which came from the east and then returned to establish the Fatimid rulers of Egypt.

The Shi'ite attack in North Africa was a mixture of Berber antagonism to the Arabs, and religious fervour. It was led in the first instance by Abu Abdallah, who mobilized the Kutama tribes from present-day Algeria in a campaign which destroyed Aghlabid power. Shi'ite beliefs were exceptionally propitious to religious devotion. Suppressed, dispersed and imprisoned by the Sunnis, the Shi'ites believed that the last descendant of Ali lived as a 'hidden Imam', waiting the moment to emerge as the *Mahdi*, the saviour of the world. Theirs was a millennial belief that the rule of the Mahdi would be a golden age of peace, justice and prosperity.

At this time – the end of the ninth century – the leader of the Shi'ite Ismaili sect, Ubaid Allah (supposedly the descendant of the seventh Imam, Ismail) lived near Homs in Syria. His missionaries spread throughout the Abbasid empire. Abu Abdallah was one of them (although he had not met Ubaid Allah at this time). Abu Abdallah, who originated in Basra, is reputed to have met members of the Kutama tribe in Mecca, and returned home with them.

His sense of mission formed a catalyst to their discontent. In a series of battles of varying fortune through the first decade of the tenth century he finally broke down the rule of the Aghlabids and entered al-Raqqada in 909. He then went in search of Ubaid Allah, who had, in response to a premature appeal several years earlier, travelled through Egypt and Tripoli, only to end up in an Aghlabid prison.

Abu Abdallah's expedition secured his release (after destroying the neighbouring kingdom of Tahert on the way). Triumphant, they returned to al-Raqqada, where Ubaid Allah declared himself Mahdi and Commander of the Faithful – a claim to leadership of the whole Muslim world.

The next years were spent by Ubaid Allah in establishing his own rule – a task made more difficult by the fact that Abu Abdallah broke with him and set up a rival Mahdi, until he was himself assassinated. Ubaid Allah also sent expeditions to conquer Egypt, none of which was successful.

Once his rule was more or less secure he moved the capital of his kingdom from Kairouan to Mahdia – a village of the Sahel which he named in accordance with his own title. Today Mahdia is a small fishing town with an attractive beach along which simple accommodation has been built for tourists. Its inhabitants retain the conservative social habits of the countryside and comment harshly on the advanced dress and behaviour of students who come from Tunis for a summer seminar. When Ubaid Allah established himself there it was probably a decayed port, with a harbour built by the Phoenicians and developed on a minor scale by the Romans.

In moving the capital to Mahdia, Ubaid Allah was following a common habit of building afresh rather than taking over the camp of his adversary. Moreover his origins and ambitions were in the east and Mahdia was a sea-port easily protected from the land, which could be developed and fortified as a military base.

Fatimid rule[2] weighed heavily on Ifriqiya. Whatever the short-comings of the Aghlabids the government of Ubaid Allah and his successors proved no less harsh than theirs; taxes were heavy and arbitrary, and the attempt to impose Shi'ite practices meant a deep disturbance of accepted theology and religion. It provoked the resistance of the religious leaders of Kairouan; more important, it aroused a fresh outburst of Kharijite revolt, led this time by a popular religious leader and fanatic named Abu Yazid. He was known as 'the man on the donkey' since he conducted his revolutionary propaganda travelling through the country, accompanied by his wife and four sons, on a donkey. A religious zealot, ascetic and poor, he rekindled the fires of Kharijism, refuelled from the Berber kingdoms to the west.

This great popular uprising had the support of the more well-to-do opponents of the Shi'ites in the towns. Coming from the west, Abu Yazid's forces won a battle near Béja, captured Tunis and occupied Kairouan. They laid a ten-month siege to Mahdia and almost succeeded in capturing it; their failure to do so was the turning point of the revolt, which gradually disintegrated over the next few years. Abu Yazid was finally captured (in 947), though, mercifully, he died of his wounds (his corpse, according to Ibn Khaldun, was flayed and the skin stuffed with straw as a toy for two monkeys in a cage). His victor – Abu Tahir Ismail, the third ruler of the dynasty, took the title of Al-Mansur (the victorious) and established a new town outside Kairouan, called Mansuriya.

The Kharijite revolt suppressed, the Fatimids at last succeeded in their ambition to establish their rule in Egypt. In 969 an army coming from the Maghreb occupied the capital and established a new capital close by the existing town of Fustat – the city of Cairo. This was the beginning of two centuries of Fatimid rule in Egypt. The Caliph lost no time in moving there, together with his treasure, government officials and the coffins of his predecessors.

Ifriqiya was left under the rule of a Berber governor – the son of a tribal leader named Ziri. This meant that the province was virtually independent, under the Zirids as tributaries of the Fatimids. Once more, it seems, Tunisia was prosperous. It is recorded that at harvest time more than a thousand camels carried away the grain from the fertile land around Béja. Irrigation and watering were developed both for crops and for gardens. The olive trees had survived the strife of the preceding years and oil was exported to the west, to Sicily and to Europe. Kairouan was by this time known as a centre for the making of carpets. Ceramics were said to be as good as those of Iraq.

The towns were enriched by the wealth of the countryside. Large tribute was paid to Cairo as it had been previously to Baghdad; but still Kairouan was able to offer a fête to Sousse, in 1050, when the party washed their hands in rose water and dried them on fine towels. Skills of government and art were imported from the east – from Iraq, Egypt and Khurasan. It was, in the words of the French authority on the period, *un opulent empire, province reculée du monde musulman, et qui empruntait à la Mésopotamie un reflet de sa beauté.*[3]

Had the Zirid kingdom survived it might have extended its civilizing influence westwards along the coast. It might have linked with the very different Muslim civilization of Spain, which, from the time of the first Berber landings in 709, had become renowned for its taste and learning in the ninth and tenth centuries – the apogee of the court of Cordoba.

Instead the Zirids made a false move. In the middle of the eleventh century they broke altogether their allegiance to Cairo, and transferred it to the Abbasids of Baghdad. Their intention was to gain greater independence from Cairo – but Baghdad was in no position to offer protection for such independence. Instead the Fatimids in Egypt despatched towards the west the Beduin tribes of the Banu Hilal and the Banu Sulaim. Their arrival in Tunisia is regarded by historians as a secular turning point in the history of the country; for they were, in the words of Ibn Khaldun, like an army of locusts. Nomadic peoples, they destroyed settled civilization except in the most protected areas of the coast. Thus in the middle of the eleventh century the society which had grown up under the Romans and substantially survived their departure was laid waste. Two centuries later Ibn Khaldun surely was thinking above all of these Beduin raiders when he wrote:

> [the Arabs] are a savage nation, fully accustomed to savagery and the things that cause it. Savagery has become their character and nature. . . . Arabs need stones to set them up as supports for their cooking pots. So, they take them from buildings which they tear down to get the stones. . . . Wood, too, is needed by them for props for their tents and for use as tent poles for their dwelling. So, they tear down roofs to get the wood for that purpose. . . . Wherever their eyes fall upon some property, furnishings or utensils, they take it. . . . There no longer exists any political [power] to protect property, and civilization is ruined.[4]

The Hilalian invasion of Tunisia destroyed sedentary civilization, by persistent demolition rather than a single battle, at a time when

Europe was acquiring renewed strength and entering a new period of expansion. The Hilalian invasion was contemporaneous with the Norman Conquest of England, and throughout Europe there was developing an intellectual renaissance, more efficient political organization, the association of Christian religion with temporal authority and political dynamism. Its new strength was accompanied by economic development and the revival of overseas trade. In Spain the easy-going relationship between Muslims and Christians began to give way to ideological and religious strife. Henceforth the hold of Muslim North Africa on the tip of Europe weakened, and Europe made a succession of incursions into north Africa – incursions of armed force, of missionaries, and of traders.

The Norman Count Roger I had begun the reconquest of Sicily in 1060. An attack on the African coast was delayed for some decades, but in 1134 the Normans occupied Jerba and so had a base for expeditions against the mainland. By 1150 they commanded the whole littoral from Tripoli to Sousse. But they made no attempt to carry their conquest inland, not did they disturb the religious and social life of those who lived in the seaports.

Their intrusion was short-lived. While the Hilalian invasion ravaged Tunisia a great nomadic religious movement had swept into Morocco from the south and established the rule of the Almoravids in Marrakesh. After three generations they in turn succumbed to a fresh wave of military and religious invasion, led by a Berber uni-tarian, Ibn Tumart and his successor Abd al-Mumin. He not only drove the Almoravids from Marrakesh, in 1147, but, with his son, extended his conquest to the eastern coast of Tunisia. The Normans were expelled – Mahdia once again served as a last stronghold, but in the end capitulated; the petty beduin 'states' were subjugated. The conquest was harsh – the remaining Christian communities were wiped out and the Jews persecuted; but for a brief time the whole of Muslim north-west Africa as well as southern Spain was brought under the rule of a single dynasty, the Almohads.

The Almohad empire lasted until 1268. Its artistic and archi-tectural achievements remain more or less intact in Marrakesh, Seville and Rabat. As far north as Burgos the Chapel of Las

Claustrillas was decorated by Muslim workmen or Arabized Christians.

To govern this empire, which until recently had been divided between unruly tribes, the Almohads followed the obvious course of appointing governors. But the sequel of such appointments could be foreseen. In the east one of them, Abdulwahid ibn Abu Hafs, established his own autonomous rule, and founded a dynasty which long outlived the Almohad empire. This was the Hafsid dynasty, which was to govern the successor to Ifriqiya and the forerunner of Tunisia for some three centuries, from 1207.

In the rest of the Maghreb the Almohad empire collapsed. It broke up first in Spain, as Valencia was lost to Aragon in 1228, and Cordoba and Seville to Castile in 1236 and 1248. Then from eastern Morocco a fresh Berber tribe, the Banu Merin, overthrew the Almohads and established their own dynasty, the Merinid. They moved the capital from Marrakesh to Fez. But they were unable to regain dominion over the Almohad empire. They suffered defeat in Spain, so that after 1269 the Kingdom of Granada alone remained under Muslim rule in Spain. Eastwards the Merinid ruler Abu al-Hassan made a successful excursion in 1348 and captured Tunis. But the dynasty was unable to establish lasting rule even as far east as Tlemcen, and was never a serious challenge to the Hafsids in Tunis.

1 Archaic Punic mask in terracotta, in
the Bardo Museum. Masks of several
different types have been found on
Phoenician sites, including Ibiza,
Sardinia and Sicily. Some are of
female faces, impassive or smiling;
others, like that shown here, are of
male, grimacing faces. Slightly less
than life-size, they could not have
been used to cover the face. They
have been found in tombs, where
they presumably gave protection to
the dead. They resemble Greek masks
of the same period, but the connection
between them has proved impossible
to establish with certainty.

2 Votive stele from the region of
Carthage (*right*). Punic stelae became
increasingly complex in the third and
second centuries BC. Moreover, their
creation survived the fall of Carthage
to Rome. The deity is framed in the
architrave of a temple, while the apex
encloses a decorated representation of
the dedicator.

3 Portrait of Virgil seated between the Muses (*left*), the papyrus on his lap inscribed with a verse from the *Aeneid* – a mosaic found at Sousse, now in the Bardo Museum.

4 (*Left, below*) Pottery bowl of the Fatimid period in the museum of Monastir. The Fatimids brought to perfection a style of painting inherited from the Abbasids of Baghdad, which has survived on pottery bowls as well as on a few outstanding buildings. It is characterized by the liveliness of its natural designs, which are lustre-painted.   5 Painted pot in the form of a bird; votive offering to Tanit. Musée Aloui, Bardo.

6 Memorial pillar from the museum of Kairouan (*above, right*), with inscription in Kufic script. It emphasizes the vertical strokes of the letters, and developed from a simple form to the more florid style, characteristic of the Fatimid period, shown here.

7 Quadrant astrolabe in the museum of Monastir (*below, right*). The use of astrolabes for navigation, survey and instruction began in Greece, was developed in the ancient world and then taken up in medieval Europe.

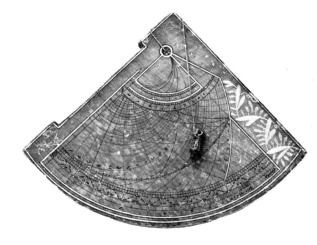

8–10 Thuburbo Majus (*left*), Dougga (*below*), and El Djem (*right*) are three of the most distinctive monuments of Roman Africa to be found in Tunisia. Thuburbo Majus retains the dominant features of a large and wealthy town, with the magnificent Corinthian columns and wide staircase of its capitol, private houses with rich mosaic floors, presses and storage for oil and grain. Dougga was constructed on a more informal plan, and its small theatre echoes the curve of the hills in which it was placed. The wedding procession which here wends its way across the site, to the thin strains of pipes, may have a direct link with the earliest citizens. By contrast the amphi-theatre of El Djem is notable for its grandeur, second only to that of Rome, having provided spectacles for some thirty thousand at a time.

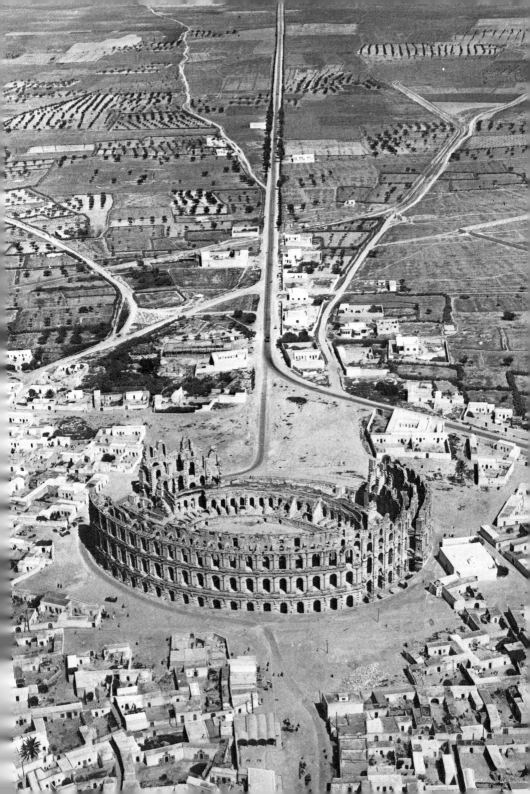

ARIADEVVS BARBARVSSA CIRTHAE, TVNE
IO. REX·AC OTOMANICAE CLASS¹¹ PRAEF

11 Khair al-Din Barbarossa, a sixteenth-century figure of wide-ranging skills and ability who broke Spanish power in North Africa, joined Algiers to the Ottoman Empire and captured Tunis. He constructed the harbour of Algiers, and was made admiral of the Ottoman fleet. He died in 1546.

12 The harbour of Tunis in 1670 (*below*).

13 Kairouan began as a citadel in the desert when the Arabs first established themselves in the west (*right*). Its period of grandeur was the ninth century under the Aghlabids; ruined by the Hilalian invasion in the eleventh century, it subsequently lost its supremacy to Tunis. It stands in the approximate centre of the country in a harsh climate, between droughts and floods. Its walls and the great mosque have been restored, and, with the minarets and domes of many smaller mosques, are evocative of a medieval religious town. It produces fine carpets.

14 Part of the Bardo Museum (*below*)
constructed in 1900 in a small palace which
had been added to the existing complex
(begun under the Hafsids) in 1831. The
patio is decorated with colonnades, fountain
and tiles of Andalusian style.

15 Charles Martial
Allemand Lavigerie
(*above*), Cardinal Arch-
bishop of Algiers and
Carthage, played a
decisive part in the
extension of French
influence in North
Africa, after mission
service in the Near East
had first awoken his
sense of vocation for
France in the Islamic
world. The order of
White Fathers, which he
founded, continue to
work in Africa,
attenuated as their
opportunities are.

4   The Hafsids and Ibn Khaldun

THE HAFSID DYNASTY maintained its rule for three centuries, until the Turkish invasion. Tunis was the capital, and under the rule of Abu Zakariya from 1228 to 1249 it was developed as fitted the inheritor of Almohad orthodoxy. The suks were constructed around the Great Mosque and the kasba was rebuilt. Kairouan in contrast never recovered its grandeur after the ravages of the Hilalians. For Tunis had become the capital at the time when the development of European commerce gave an importance to the ports which no inland city could rival. A trade treaty was signed with Pisa in 1157 – possibly the oldest commercial treaty to be signed between North Africa and Christian Europe. Genoa, Pisa, Marseilles, Venice were quick to develop their trade, and in May 1225 the Seigneurie of Venice fixed the days of departure for ships going to Tunis, Bougie and Ceuta. Fresh treaties were signed by Abu Zakariya, and the Pisans seem first to have been given extensive privileges in the right to reside in major ports as well as Tunis, to have a chapel and ceme-tery wherever they had a funduk (or factory) and to have audience of the prince or the local governor once a month. In this way the pattern of a new Tunisia was rapidly being shaped.

Abu Zakariya's successor, Abu Abdallah, extended the success of the regime still further. Having survived an insurrection at the beginning of the reign he took the title of Caliph, Amir al-Muminin, and the surname al-Mustansir in 1253. His claim to Muslim leader-ship was the more convincing since at this time the Abbasid Caliphate at Baghdad was proving vulnerable to the encroachments of the Mongols, while the major towns of Muslim Spain – including

Seville and Cadiz – had fallen to the Castilians. The building and embellishment of Tunis proceeded accordingly, and the capital grew richer from the influx of refugees from Spain, giving its society a new brilliance and its buildings a fresh beauty.

The height of Abu Abdallah's fame came a few years later. He received letters of homage from Fez and Tlemcen. More important, as the Abbasid Caliphate finally collapsed before the Mongols in 1258 al-Mustansir was briefly recognized as Caliph even by Mecca and Cairo.

Meanwhile he maintained good relations with the cities and powers of Europe. He received a mission from King Haakon the Old of Norway, which was presumably followed by a commercial treaty. Good relations generally existed with Aragon. Localized disputes did not disturb a sound relationship with the Italian cities. Christian missionaries were active in the Hafsid state, and diplomatic relations had been established with Paris.

Yet it was in these circumstances of a developing trade and cultural relationship between North Africa and Europe that Saint Louis of France led a crusade to Tunis. The expedition, which resulted in his own death, appears as a strange aberration. In March 1270 he left Paris for Aigues Mortes to embark on his third crusade towards the Holy Land. The fleet put in to Cagliari in Sardinia where it was joined by others who had left from Marseilles. It set sail again, towards Palestine or Egypt; but then turned south towards Tunis.

Saint Louis' motives remain uncertain. If he had conquered north-west Africa he might have been in a stronger position to attack Egypt – although the knights of Europe were scarcely equipped for or accustomed to the kind of desert campaigning which took Arab armies so swiftly along the North African coast. It was therefore scarcely worth engaging in a campaign so distant from the ultimate objective, and it is generally assumed that Saint Louis was persuaded that al-Mustansir would easily be converted to Christianity – a supposition for which there is no evidence in the scant records that remain on the Muslim side.

The expedition landed without resistance at Carthage in July. There it waited, having received a message from the King's brother,

Charles, asking that the offensive should be delayed until he arrived. In the hot sun dysentery swept through the crusaders' camp. The king's younger brother and the papal legate died, as did many humbler men. Saint Louis was already ill, and on 25 August he too succumbed.

After his death the conflict dissipated itself. His brother Charles arrived from Sicily at the moment of his death and took over command. Two indecisive battles were fought – al-Mustansir's forces were defeated, but the crusaders lacked the energy or resources to push further inland. Both sides continued to be ravaged by dysentery. A peace treaty was signed and an indemnity payable to the crusaders as well as tribute to Charles as king of Sicily agreed. The crusade withdrew, and a more normal sequence was resumed of trading relationships with the Christian powers of Europe interrupted from time to time by petty warfare.

Yet it was scarcely possible for a Christian king and a saint, a leader of the crusades, to have died and been buried at Carthage without legends growing up around the event. In Tunisian folklore it came to be said that he had not died, but had been converted to Islam and spent the rest of his life as a Muslim holy man – the saint of Sidi bou Said. For France in later centuries a new episode had been added to the history of Christian North Africa, on which, in the nineteenth century, Cardinal Lavigerie was to build his plans for the conversion of a continent.

A generation after Saint Louis' abortive crusade occurred a quite different attempt to convert Muslim North Africa to Christianity. In 1292 a Catalan missionary disembarked at Tunis. He was Raimon Lull, who was born in Majorca some sixty years earlier and who, after an early life of worldly pleasure, became converted to a mystical and evangelical form of Christianity. Living in the borderlands between the Islamic, Arab empire and that of Christian Europe he conceived it to be his mission to convert Muslims to Christianity. He learned Arabic, and persuaded the King of Majorca to establish a monastery at Miramar, where he taught Arabic and philosophy.

He received little support and won little popularity for his efforts. When he went to Tunis in 1292, after a year of indecision and heart-searching, he was a lone figure embarking on a single-handed mission of conversion. It was not that Christians were unknown in Tunis – on the contrary they were established there as traders, and the Hafsid ruler, Abu Hafs, had a Christian bodyguard whose captain was appointed by the King of Aragon. But these were self-contained communities, engaging in the practice of their own religion without seeking to convert others. Raimon Lull, in contrast, sought out the leading Muslim teachers in order to enter into controversy with them. The teachers and scholars of Tunis were in no way averse to such an exercise and probably took great pleasure in theological argument and disputation, without ever coming near to conversion. Raimon Lull believed that in the time of the prophets men had been converted by faith, in the time of Christ and the apostles by miracles – but in an age of reason they could only be converted when their error was demonstrated by rational argument.

But not all Muslims were as content to argue as were the Muslim philosophers. The argument continued for the best part of a year, but in the end Lull was denounced and the ruler pressed to execute him. However Abu Hafs had no intention of endangering his diplomatic relations with Aragon and the other Christian states by putting to death a wild missionary. He ordered his imprisonment, and after various diversions Lull was deported.

His sense of mission continued unabated. He still sought to interest the Christian princes in his cause, without success. He developed further his own mystical theories and utopian philosophy, and re-turned twice to North Africa. In 1307 he sailed to Bougie (Bijana in Algeria) where the pattern repeated itself though with more violence. His offer to prove the truth of Christianity was taken up by the Mufti, who argued with him in his house; but when Lull left the house he was stoned by the crowd, and imprisoned for six months. His third mission came in 1314 – when he was nearly eighty. The end of this mission was also the end of his life – although the details and the date of his death are obscure. It seems likely that he was once again maltreated by the crowd, and although he almost certainly died when he was home in Majorca he inevitably became a local martyr.

Raimon Lull's missions were no more than a colourful episode in the history of the Hafsid monarchy and its relations with Europe. When the Hafsid princes of Tunis were at the height of their power they governed the area which comprises Tunisia at the present time, together with Tripoli and the region of Constantine, across the present frontier with Algeria. In the interior the limits of their rule were not clearly defined, since government was exercised over tribes rather than countryside.

In these circumstances political stability depended entirely on the success and skill of the ruler; as soon as they weakened so did the area of his authority. A natural geographical division always opened the possibility of the establishment of an independent political unit based on Bougie. Further to the west the Merinid kingdom of Fez was ready to fill a vacuum of power in Tunisia. The desert tribes thrived on instability – ever ready to assist in revolt and be rewarded thereby, but intractable to settled government. Across the Mediterranean the small Christian states – Aragon, Pisa, Genoa, Provence, Sicily – all had interests and ambitions in north-west Africa. Singly or in combination these rival forces could undermine the authority of Tunis.

Thus it was that the grandeur of the dynasty, which had seemed so secure at the end of the life of al-Mustansir, disintegrated immediately after his death in 1277. He was succeeded by his son, but within two years al-Mustansir's brother led a rebellion against him, with the support of Peter III of Aragon. Once in power Abu Ishaq broke with his ally. But his power was circumscribed, Peter of Aragon supported another rival at Constantine, and Abu Ishaq ran into trouble with the Arab tribes. In 1284 Abu Hafs was carried to power by the Banu-Sulaim tribe, and managed to rule for more than a decade. He had to pay heavily for this relative stability by rewarding the Arabs with the rent and taxes of certain of the districts of Sfax and Jerid.

Nor could Abu Hafs do anything to prevent a fleet from Sicily, commanded by the Aragonese Roger de Loria, from occupying Jerba in 1284 after a brief bombardment. Although the action had not been directed by the King of Aragon it was followed by the negotiation of a new treaty under which Abu Hafs paid tribute to the Crown of Aragon as ruler of Sicily. In spite of this Roger de Loria carried out a fresh raid on the Kerkenna islands and the whole eastern coast in 1287. Meanwhile Abu Hafs' nephew Abu Zakariya established himself as an independent ruler in Bougie and encroached increasingly on his authority in the west, to the extent that the ruler of Gabès defected to him.

When Abu Hafs died in 1295 he was succeeded by a boy of fifteen, Abu Asida. Although his first act was to have Abu Hafs' son killed, to eliminate a possible rival, he was unable to reunite the kingdom. For three-quarters of a century the rivalry between Tunis and Bougie continued, with brief intermissions. The division of the eastern Maghreb was a tempting prize for the neighbouring rulers of Fez and Tlemcen. In 1347 and again in 1357 Merinid princes invaded eastwards and captured power in Tunis as well as Bougie. They did so with the help of the tribes; but having done so they were unable to solve the problem of government over those who had been their allies, and their authority disintegrated.

In this turbulent atmosphere lived the historian and philosopher Ibn Khaldun – a man whose contribution to human thought was and is justly commemorated in Tunisia. He was an intellectual in politics, who believed that a study of philosophy would enable him to prescribe the proper course of action to rulers; and he was an historian who turned to the past to discover the principles underlying human experience. Largely unsuccessful in the Arab west, discouraged and frustrated by the insecurity and instability of its politics, he emigrated (at the age of fifty) to Cairo, where he completed the writing of his major works – while still holding judicial and political office.

His life illustrates well the unity of the medieval Islamic world – and its insecurity. His family came from Arabia and settled in southern Spain, where his ancestors were among the leading families of Seville. Before the fall of Seville to the Christians, Ibn Khaldun's grandfather emigrated to North Africa, and Ibn Khaldun himself was born in Tunis in May 1332. He grew to manhood under conditions of upheaval which were extreme even for north-west Africa.

The Hafsids were twice under attack by the Merinid dynasty of Fez, and the Black Death devastated Tunis in 1348-9, carrying off both Ibn Khaldun's parents. Thus deprived, and in the pursuit of a more settled scholarly environment, he spent a decade at the Merinid court in Fez, where he brought up his family. He was given minor official employment; but he entered into a lasting friendship with the Hafsid Abu Abdallah (who was in Fez) which his princely employer could only regard as dangerous, since he was planning a fresh attack on the Hafsids. Ibn Khaldun was imprisoned for twenty-one months.

By the time he was released Fez was as disturbed as Tunis had been, and he sought refuge in Granada, where he was welcomed by the ruler, Muhammad V, and his scholarly prime minister Ibn al-Khatib. His stay lasted only three years before political jealousies induced him to leave and return to North Africa (in 1365) without finding any solution to his predicament.

He was always attracted by the opportunities of political office. He had a broad view of political events, a sharp mind and great ability in negotiation, and a firm conviction that what he had learned from scholarly studies was relevant to political action. But for the exercise of these talents he was dependent on the good will – and the good fortune – of princes, whose futures were difficult to predict, and any one of whom, by conferring a favour on him, placed him in jeopardy with a rival. It seemed inevitable that a man of his ability should be caught between the conflicting ambitions and varying fortunes of rival dynasties – the Merinids of Fez, Abu Hammu of Tlemcen, the Hafsids of Tunis.

Yet the work which he undertook for such rulers widened and deepened his knowledge of human customs and behaviour. Twice he accepted missions – on the behalf first of Abdul Aziz of Fez then of Abu Hammu of Tlemcen – to the Arab tribes, with the object of winning their support and so tipping the balance of power in his prince's favour.

On the second occasion however he did not complete his mission. Fatigued and dispirited by the frustrating and dangerous business of politics, he accepted the hospitality of Awlad Arif, brought his family to the castle of Ibu Salamah (near Oran) and spent three years there in quiet and scholarly work completing the introduction to his history of the world.

'I completed it', he said,

> in that remarkable manner to which I was inspired by that retreat, with words and ideas pouring into my head like cream into a churn, until the finished product was ready.[1]

The words and the ideas derived from his awareness of the way in which political and social events take place. His knowledge of men's behaviour was drawn from direct experience. He was in consequence profoundly impatient with the improbabilities of the anecdotal chronicles which passed as history. Legends had gained currency and authority because they were accepted and reported by eminent men of learning: but Ibn Khaldun subjected them to critical scrutiny, testing them against the possibilities and probabilities of human experience. But the skills which made him a good historian also meant that he could not remain long on the sidelines of politics – even though the turbulence of the political world, and his own ability, would never give him peace. However he tried to resolve the tensions of his life, he was too important a figure to be left out of the political calculations of others.

After a long illness at Ibu Salamah he returned to Tunis to continue his work and to teach. Finding himself once again surrounded by intrigue and suspicion he begged leave to go on a pilgrimage to Mecca as a means of escaping to Egypt, where he arrived in December 1383 – a journey which indirectly led to the loss of his family, drowned at sea when they left Tunis to join him.

In Cairo he was able to pursue his scholarly and teaching career. At the same time he was appointed *cadi,* an office which he held on and off, according to political circumstance, until his death. There was, too, a more colourful episode during his life in Egypt. The Mameluke rulers of Egypt were engaged in the defence of the Islamic world against the Mongol invasions of Tamerlane, and Ibn Khaldun took the opportunity to accompany his ruler on a military expedition to Syria. On the second occasion that he did so he was besieged in

Damascus. Learning that Tamerlane had enquired about him, he had himself lowered from the walls of the city and sought out the Mongol leader in his camp. There he stayed for thirty-five days. He fended off Tamerlane's questions (designed to discover the weakness of Egypt as a prelude to extending his conquest) and eventually secured leave for himself and his companions to return to Cairo in peace.[2]

In spite of the upheavals of so adventurous a political career Ibn Khaldun left to the world a great monument of historical study, the *Kitab al-Ibar*. It comprises a discursive introduction, the *Muqaddimah*, and the historical volumes subsequently translated into French as the *Histoire des Berbères*. In addition he wrote the history of the pre-Islamic world and of eastern Islam. In this part of his work he was forced to rely on secondary sources, and his account has been superseded by the discoveries of later historians. But what he writes of north-west Africa, especially of the Arab tribes, derives from direct and first-hand knowledge so that it remains an unsurpassed source for the period.

The whole work provides an immense field for scholarly research. The intellectual environment in which he wrote was one where Arab philosophers had taken over and reinterpreted the classical works of ancient Greece. The writings of Plato and Aristotle, the product of a political community based on the city-states of Greece, had been the starting point of Farabi, Avicenna, and Averroes, working in the desert and city community of the Muslim world. Ibn Khaldun's work is therefore as interesting for the historian of philosophy as for the historian concerned with the accuracy of his political history.

Of immense value to scholars, the *Muqaddimah* is vigorous, fascinating and full of stimulus for the general reader. As we have seen he subjected existing historical accounts to the scrutiny of common sense. But he also sought an additional guarantee of authenticity, and found it in 'the science of culture'. By this he meant a study of human social behaviour, designed to provide a framework against which historical reports could be checked for their probable accuracy. His generalizations were themselves derived from empirical observation and investigation; and what he set out to do, undeterred by the magnitude of his task, was to construct a corpus of historical knowledge – indeed of knowledge in general – against which the authenticity of supposed accounts could be judged. In his own words:

the scholar . . . needs to know the principles of politics, the [true] nature of existing things, and the differences among nations, places and periods with regard to ways of life, character, qualities, customs, sects, schools and everything else. . . . He must know the causes of the similarities in certain cases and of the differences in others. He must be aware of the differing origins and beginnings of different dynasties and religious groups, as well as the reasons and incentives that brought them into being and the circumstances and history of the persons who supported them. His goal must be to have complete knowledge of the reasons for every happening, and to be acquainted with the origin of every event. Then, he must check transmitted information with the basic principles he knows.[3]

He argues the case, to use the words of R. G. Collingwood centuries later, for the study of history as an autonomous discipline – different from rhetoric, and different from the prescriptive science of politics:

because politics is concerned with the administration of home or city in accordance with ethical and philosophical requirements, for the purpose of directing the mass toward a behaviour that will result in the preservation and permanence of the [human] species.[4]

His breadth of vision saw the full extent of what he was proposing. He was aware of individual peculiarities, but equally that men live in society and have 'group feeling'; he saw that men's lives are determined by the way in which they make their living as well as the way they are ruled; that their fortunes are related to world politics – and that a study of world history provides a gauge by which to check the history of smaller units. 'It should be known', he wrote,

that history, in matter of fact, is information about human social organization, which itself is identical with world civilization. It deals with such conditions affecting the nature of civilization as, for instance, savagery and sociability, group feelings, and the different ways by which one group of human beings achieves superiority over another. It deals with royal authority and the dynasties that result [in this manner] and with the various ranks that exist between them. [It further deals] with the different kinds of gainful occupations and ways of making a living, with the sciences and crafts that human beings pursue as part of their activities and efforts, and with all the other institutions that originate in civilization through its very nature.[5]

The world in which Ibn Khaldun lived was not one of slow change, far less a static society, or one of steady progress. On the grand scale it was one of great sweeping movements – the creation of the Muslim empire, now challenged by the Mongols at the gates of Damascus. In the smaller dimensions of Tunisia, towns and settled communities were under constant threat from the desert; buildings were constructed in times of peace and torn down by nomadic invaders. It is understandable that in these surroundings Ibn Khaldun should generalize his observations of the rise and fall of kingdoms, and develop a cyclical view of change.

Dynasties, he said, have a natural life, of coming into being and then decaying, consequent on human characteristics. In a single family the prestige of a dynasty lasts only four generations. The first – the 'builder of authority' – is aware of how his authority was built and he therefore works to maintain it; his son benefits from personal contact with his father, but has learned from study rather than first-hand experience; the third generation, inheriting power and authority, is necessarily imitative; the fourth yet more inferior.

In the same way it is natural for peoples to achieve great things and then decay. In the desert they acquire group feeling and have as their ambition the establishment of cities and a sedentary life. Once they have achieved this they then fall prey to luxurious living and bring about their own destruction. Thus 'sedentary culture is the goal of civilization. It means the end of its life span and brings about its corruption.'

This description of a cyclical movement in history has attracted frequent comment from those who have studied Ibn Khaldun's work, and rightly so. But it is certainly no more important than the contribution he made to the science of historical study through his aware-ness of its methods and standards; or indeed of the historical writing itself. What he had achieved was to write philosophy and history which was closely related to his own background and beliefs, deeply infused with the faith and conviction of a Muslim: yet at the same time having a critical approach and a breadth of vision which makes it of universal value and interest.

As if to belie Ibn Khaldun's sombre predictions about the life of dynasties the Hafsid rulers regained their vigour and restored the prestige and power of their kingdom. The Aragonese had been unable to retain their hold over Jerba, which was recaptured in 1335. As the fourteenth century drew to a close it was the North African kingdoms which raided the shipping of the Christian states in various acts of more or less encouraged piracy. So much was this so that in 1390 a Venetian–Genoese fleet, with the support of some French vessels, was sent against Mahdia to quell piracy based on that port. The attack failed, the fortifications of the port (to which Froissart refers in his history) once again proving too tough for the invaders.

The victor in this battle was Abu Faris Abdul Aziz, who succeeded to the dynasty in 1394 and enjoyed a brilliant reign for forty years. In the early years of his rule he extended the work begun by his father. He established his own authority over local rulers, who habitually set up petty princedoms whenever there was no strong central power – at Tripoli, Gafsa, Tozeur and Kiskra. He sent expeditions into the more hilly and desert regions of his territory – although it was virtually impossible to establish more than a short-lived authority there. During one of these expeditions – towards Ghadamès in the Libyan desert – he had to avert a palace revolution at home. He succeeded in overcoming the dangers, which had been so threatening for his predecessors, from the combined power of a pretender and the Arab tribes and extended his rule westwards, establishing an important post west of Bougie – at Algiers.

The success of Abu Faris was attributable not only to his military and campaigning skill but to his qualities as a good Muslim ruler. He showed great respect for the religious leaders under his rule. That he was able to do so suggests a greater acceptance of orthodox religion in previous centuries. He even tried to strengthen Sunnite orthodoxy in Jerba, which retained – as it does to this day – strong elements of Kharijism. He celebrated the birthday of the Prophet – a practice which had only begun in the Maghreb in the previous century. Like the Aghlabids in an earlier century, he carried out improvements in the provision of water – a work of religious as well as purely practical importance. He suppressed taxes which were not sanctioned by the Koran, and which weighed heavily on commerce and crafts.

Abu Faris was now in the ascendant, while his rivals in the west were in decline. The pattern of the previous century was therefore reversed. Abu Faris occupied Tlemcen, setting up a vassal state there, and advanced almost as far as Fez. He also intervened actively in the affairs of the dying princedom of Granada. The Christian reconquest of the Iberian peninsula complete, the Spanish and Portuguese kingdoms established themselves on the Moroccan coast – in spite of the assistance which Abu Faris gave to the Moroccans, enlarging his navy and promoting attacks on the Christian fleets.

Reprisals inevitably ensued. Alphonse V of Aragon's fleet raided the Kerkennas in 1424, and Hafsid ships counter-attacked against the coast of Italy and Malta. In 1432 Alphonse conducted an attack on Jerba, but Abu Faris led his troops in battle and saved the island. The Aragonese had cut the causeway, but Muslim troops counter-attacked at low tide and the Spaniards were forced to retire. Victory of this sort reinforced the dubious prestige which the Hafsids enjoyed in the Italian republics as well as Aragon. Piracy flourished. Ships were captured and their cargoes taken; their crews were taken prisoner and held to ransom. In 1428 a Hafsid fleet carried off peaceful inhabitants from the isle of Capri; two years later they captured Genoese ships in harbour at Bougie, along with their passengers. As a result negotiations were constantly in course in an attempt to arrive at terms and conditions of a peaceful relationship – the Hafsids reaping the maximum material benefit from their treaties, their own security guaranteed for the time being by the weakness and rivalries of their victims. Small wonder that the government of Genoa and the King of Aragon in turn referred to Abu Faris as *rex opulentissimus, prudentissimus et magna fama in toto orbe clarissimus* and *Barbarorum omnium regum potentissimus.*[7]

Abu Faris died in the middle of the new campaign to retain his authority at Tlemcen. Narrowly averting the familiar problem of the succession, the dynasty remained in power and kept its authority and prestige through another half-century. The sultan's grandson – born to a concubine of Christian origin from Valence – died of illness after a brief reign. His half-brother, Utman, was declared his successor, and although he was only sixteen he succeeded in maintaining his authority against the intrigues of his uncles, the natural rebelliousness of the tribes and the fissiparous tendencies of regions and cities. Becoming ruler in 1435 he survived until 1494.

During these sixty years Utman kept intact the power and authority he had inherited from his grandfather. In spite of the growing power of the European states his relations with them followed a similar pattern – exchange of acts of piracy, followed by negotiations to settle accounts and restore relations – a curious *modus vivendi* when Christian subjects were responsible for the major part of Tunisia's trade, operating as they did from their 'factories' in the ports, while shipping and even citizens living near the coast were in constant danger of piratical attack.

But when Utman died the Hafsid kingdom disintegrated. Nor, as had happened in previous centuries, was this accompanied by the rise of a new North African power to the west. On the contrary, the decline of the Merinids and their successors the Banu Wattas made Morocco vulnerable to the attacks of Portuguese and Spaniards. In the east the island of Jerba, almost a barometer of the strength of rival powers in this part of the Mediterranean, fell to the Sicilians from 1497 until they were withdrawn in 1500.

But while the centuries of Hafsid rule lasted, Tunisia had increasingly acquired a character of its own. It would be entirely anachronistic to suggest that it had become a nation, but three centuries under a single dynasty, the last under two eminent rulers, had nonetheless given some sort of unity – especially to that part of Ifriqiya which became Tunisia, when the western province of Constantine, around Bougie and Tripolitania, were severed from it.

The great division in the population followed from the natural division between the area of settlement and the steppe and desert which formed the home of nomadic tribes. But there was for the most part much intermingling across these areas, and the distinction between Arabs and Berbers had, by the end of the Hafsid period, become very blurred. The first Arabs to arrive in Ifriqiya had lived in towns and in their citadels; they were not sufficiently numerous to have a major impact on the existing population. It was the invasion of the Banu Hilal and the Banu Sulaim which spread an Arab population through the countryside. Ibn Khaldun refers to these and related tribes when he speaks of Arabs, but the intermarriage which makes the distinction between Arabs and Berbers meaningless in the greater part of Tunisia today was already taking place. As it did so the language and religion of the Arabs predominated – Berber almost disappeared and Kharijism became a minority sect. The modern dialect of the Tunisian countryside has been traced to that of the invading tribes.

The Berber population only remained intact where it was safe-guarded by natural barriers, and for the most part these were areas which later, under Turkish rule, became part of Algeria – particularly in the Aurès mountains and Kabylia. In Tunisia the most important remnants of a Berber-speaking population were to be found in Jerba, in the poorest part of the island, separated from their fellows by their attachment to schismatic religion as well as by language. In the island as a whole a distinctive physical structure still remains – the cranium of a Jerbian is round in contrast to the longer form of the Arabs. At the present time the most Berber of the Jerbians still live in the area described as their residual home by Ibn Khaldun.[8]

Meanwhile Tunisia benefited greatly from an influx of refugees. The Spanish *reconquista* brought the highly civilized and cultivated Muslims from Spain to North Africa. The re-imposition of Christian rule brought anti-semitism with it, and many Jews left Spain, a large proportion going first to Leghorn and then later re-emigrating to North Africa. The Jews of Jerba, whose origin is lost in antiquity, retained their small and closely enclosed community. But in all the coastal towns of Tunisia a new Jewish population grew up. Inevitably the Jews formed a community apart. They were tolerated by their Muslim rulers, but subjected to discrimination of varying intensity. Long established practice in Islam – maintained intermittently – permitted the requirement that Jews should bear a distinctive sign on their clothing: in the fifteenth century the Jewish immigrants coming from Leghorn – the *livournais* – appear to have worn a cap which indicated their superiority (to which they themselves attached great importance) over the earlier communities. As might be expected the Jews lived in their own quarters of the towns – although they were probably not closely confined to them.

Christians too created their own communities. Indigenous Christian communities had by now completely disappeared, and the Christian population was one of immigrants from Europe. Christianity for those engaged in commerce was no doubt more often a matter of national and political allegiance than of devotion.

Meanwhile the Muslim population had, throughout north-west Africa, developed its distinctive religious and social organization. Its central feature was the prestige acquired by marabuts and the development of shrines associated with them. In any religious society holy men are accorded reverence and acquire a reputation for saintliness. It is common experience too that such reverence gives rise to a puritanical reaction which reaffirms the separation between the two planes of human and divine existence and regards as sinful arrogance any claim to lessen the gap between them.

In north-west Africa the holy life was at first lived in the *ribats*, by men who were ascetic and devout, military monks for whom the propagation of religion by the sword was a holy pursuit. Abd Allah bin Yasin led such a movement amongst the Sinhadja of Mauritania, and Almoravid rule was the final development of it. But as time passed, the institution of the *ribat* lost its strength and came to be replaced by religious life centred around a holy man or teacher – a marabut. When the holy man died he was buried under a dome, or at least given a small wall to protect his tomb, and a local cult grew up round the shrine.

Some of the outstanding saints of North Africa have authenticated historical existence. Others are the subject of legends with as much verisimilitude as that of St George and the dragon. Important towns have their patron saints – Sidi 'l Salah, the companion of the Prophet, at Kairouan, the woman saint Lalla A'isha al-Mannubyya of Tunis. More modestly, at least every town and village named 'Sidi . . .' acknowledges its saintly patron. The story of the life of such saints is deeply entwined with folklore, and no doubt the existence of some is fictitious – in the same way that Oxford, having once had an 'Old Gate', acquired a 'St Aldate' and a church named after that saint.

The small white domes which mark the tomb of the marabut are a familiar part of the North African scene, in Tunisia and even more to the west. The life of the *zawiya* or shrine is an integral part of village life. In the Arab east a *zawiya* (properly the corner of a room) is a small mosque or prayer room: in north-west Africa it is a complex which has grown up round the mausoleum of a saint. The *zawiya* might include a room for prayer, with a mihrab, the tomb of the saint, a room for the recitation of the Koran, a Koranic school and rooms for travellers, pilgrims and students. Nearby there might be a cemetery for those who had expressed a wish to be buried there. After the death of the marabut his direct descendant would be in charge of the shrine as *muqaddam*. He would administer revenues coming to the shrine from voluntary gifts and from land attached to the shrine in mortmain – the kind of trust known in the Arab east as *waqf* and in north-west Africa as *habous*. With his family he would be likely to inherit the *baraka* or prestige which emanates from divine selection.

It is easy to see how important a place the *zawiya* could come to occupy in religious and social life. It provided a centre of mystical practices and at the same time made religion more accessible to a population which sought solace from adversity in superstition, folk-lore and immemorial beliefs inherited from pagan days. The dis-tribution of the revenues played and still plays a part in village welfare; the prestige of the *muqaddam* is still an essential part of the structure of hierarchy in the village. The ceremonies surrounding the *zawiya*, the beliefs and hopes attached to them make life worth living when otherwise it is little more than a struggle for existence.

5 Ottoman rule: Tunisia of the Beys

AFTER THE DEATH OF UTMAN in 1494 the decline of the Hafsid dynasty was accompanied by the extension of a fresh dominion over the greater part of north-west Africa, and Tunisia as well as Tripoli and Algeria became Regencies of the Ottoman empire. Ottoman rule was established on the borders of Morocco, some seventy years after the fall of Constantinople (1453). This extension of the Ottoman empire along the shores of the Mediterranean depended on the initiative and skill of a family of privateers, at a time when the expansive energies of Suleiman the Magnificent were fully engaged in defeating the Hungarians at the battle of Mohacs (1526) and advancing to the gates of Vienna.

The privateers came to be known as the Barbarossas, although the epithet is properly applied to only one of them, Khair al-Din. They came from Mitylene, which had been an established base for Catalan, Sicilian and Italian pirates. But they were the sons of a former janissary, who had set up as a potter after his retirement.[1] The brothers have sometimes been depicted by their adversaries as ignorant and blood-thirsty pirates. In fact they were gifted and scholarly men, engaged in the honourable and established career of privateering, not piracy. Khair al-Din spoke French, Spanish and Italian as well as Greek, Arabic and Turkish. He constructed the mole of the harbour of Algiers and is said to have founded a college at Constantinople. He defeated the Spaniards in what were virtually their home waters, with minimal aid from the Ottomans fifteen hundred miles away; and his achievements were recognized by Suleiman, who appointed him Admiral in Chief of his fleet, in 1533.

The early career of the Barbarossa brothers is inevitably obscure. It appears however that the oldest of them, Aruj, was given a privateering commission by merchants of Constantinople. Soon after 1500, in pursuit of this commission, he established himself on Jerba (after the Sicilian withdrawal). There he was joined by his brother, Khair al-Din (a third brother, Elias, was killed in a battle off Egypt while the fourth, Isaak, stayed in Mitylene).

A Turkish outpost, having tenuous links with Constantinople, had thus been established in the western Mediterranean. This significant event happened at the same time as the Spaniards extended their conquests across the straits of Gibraltar. A combination of religious zeal, the pursuit of material gain, strategic rivalry with other European states and easy conquest provided a powerful motive for expansion. While the Portuguese took Mazagan, Tangier and Ceuta the Spaniards occupied Melilla (1497), Oran, Algiers and Tripoli. They encountered little resistance and would no doubt have expanded further had it not been for the more exacting conflict in which they were engaged with their European rivals.

From Jerba Aruj launched an expedition to Algiera, and twice laid siege, unsuccessfully, to Bougie. His forces totally depleted, he established himself at Jijelli, on the eastern point of the Gulf of Bougie. In spite of the failure to capture Bougie the prestige of Aruj and his brother Khair al-Din was sufficient for the people of Algiers to appeal to them, in 1516, for assistance to oust the Spaniards. The campaign which resulted was drawn out. Aruj was killed, probably in 1518, leaving Khair al-Din to continue the battle. With assistance from Turkey he succeeded in capturing the island fort of Penon, off Algiers, in 1529.[2] Algiers itself now passed under Ottoman rule, which was to last until the French occupation in 1830.

The capture of Algiers by Barbarossa meant a decisive change in the balance of power in the Mediterranean: the Ottomans had established themselves as far west as Barcelona and Paris. More important, they had passed a decisive frontier from the moment they pressed beyond the narrow seas between Sicily and Tunis. So, soon after the reconquest of its own territory, Spain was confronted with the intrusion of another great power into her own maritime sphere.

The ports and coasts of Tunisia thus became the front line between Spain and its allies, and the Turks.

So it was that Barbarossa's initial capture of Tunis lasted only until the next year, when Charles V – the last great medieval emperor pursuing the ideal of a universal empire – counterattacked and regained Tunis in 1535. A few years later however, in 1541, a similar attack on Algiers failed, and Charles V was forced to concentrate his energies on his European conflicts. In spite of the capture of Tunis, his hold on North Africa therefore remained tenuous. As ruler of Tunis he restored the Hafsid Moulay Hassan – a monarch who had never been popular, and was less so after the massacre with which he celebrated his return. Only with assistance from the Genoese admiral, Prince Andrea Doria, did he succeed in extending his domain down the coast to Sfax. But the southern interior of the country escaped from his control and a theocratic republic was established under the religious leader Shabbiya at Kairouan. Soon afterwards Moulay Hassan was overthrown by his son, Moulay Hamida, who installed himself in his father's place (and put his father's eyes out).

If the waters around Tunisia were the frontier between Spain and Turkey, they were also seas in which a small naval force could operate effectively and independently. For although great strategic conflicts were fought in the Mediterranean in this century, the art of navigation remained primitive, and the sea was still divided into numerous smaller seas, over which a successful captain could establish his supremacy.

One such sea was in the gulf formed where Tunisia now adjoins Libya – known as the Little Syrte. It was controlled by a Turkish captain named Draghut. He was an adventurer of Greek origin, born at the beginning of the century, who had spent four years in Genoese galleys before being ransomed by Barbarossa (in 1544). In 1550 he established himself on Jerba; but he was a welcome tenant neither with the Jerbian notables nor with the Shabbiyas in the interior. When opportunity offered he moved his base to the small town of Africa, north of Sfax – important at the time of the Fatimids, but now an almost empty village.

The growing strength of Draghut had largely neutralized Charles

V's restoration of the Hafsids. The Spaniards held La Goulette, the fort at the mouth of the Lake of Tunis. But this was insufficient to prevent Draghut holding sea traffic through the Sicilian narrows to ransom, or raiding the coasts of Sicily as he chose. In counterattack, Charles V launched an expedition in 1550 under the leadership of Prince Andrea Doria to capture Africa. The expedition was long, arduous, and in the end successful only to the extent that it took Africa – not Draghut, who moved eastwards and the next year seized Tripoli. A Sicilian force was established temporarily at Africa – but at Tripoli Draghut had ended two decades of rule by the Knights of St John, and brought the town under Turkish rule which was to last until 1911.

There was soon no obstacle to his return to Tunisia. Africa was abandoned a few years after its occupation by Doria's forces and Draghut overcame the resistance of his former opponents. He defeated the sheikhs of Jerba and the neighbouring mainland, took Gafsa and overthrew the independent republic of Kairouan. His sea power could not destroy the strength which his rivals drew from the land; but he was able to re-establish his base on Jerba.

In the year that he did so Charles V of Spain died. He was succeeded by Philip II, one of whose first acts was to make peace with France at Cateau-Cambrésis. This truce in the war in Europe opened the way to a fresh attack on the power of Turkey. Once again an expedition was launched against Draghut, but it was even more disastrous than the first. Initially the circumstances appeared favourable and the potential reward great. Draghut, it was known, had to dissipate his energies to maintain his dominion over his defeated antagonists in the interior – especially the Amir Shabbiya, whose religious authority was great – *quasi come il Papa tra Christiani*.[3] The Knights of Malta stood to gain as much from the recovery of Tripoli as Philip did from a victory over the Turks so early in his reign. But this did not diminish the difficulties of mobilizing a fleet and a landing force against an enemy of unknown strength – and using it to catch Draghut. The fleet at last left Syracuse at the beginning of December 1559; it was caught by storms, took refuge at Malta and finally reached Jerba at the beginning of March 1560.

Before it did so, Draghut had slipped away to Sicily. The expedition ought perhaps to have pursued him there, but Jerba itself, its oil and its wool were too rich and too tempting a prize to forego. And so it was that the Christian force, engaged in raiding the island, was caught in a state of complete unpreparedness when Draghut returned. His fleet, reinforced by that of his ally Piali Pasha, descended on the invaders. Of the forty-eight galleys in the Christian fleet twenty-eight were destroyed. Five thousand prisoners were taken and the small garrison on Jerba massacred – their bones heaped into a tower of skulls, which remained as a gruesome monument until 1846.

The disaster of Jerba was a grievous blow to Philip II and struck heavily at his prestige in the early years of his reign. It was followed in 1569 by a further extension of Ottoman power as the new ruler of Algiers, Eulj Ali, mounted an expedition by land into Tunisia. The meagre authority of Moulay Hamida collapsed in the face of invasion, Moulay Hamida himself sought refuge with the Spaniards and a *caid* named Ramdan was installed in his place.

La Goulette remained in Spanish hands, rebuilt and fortified. It is known that Philip II spent 50,000 ducats on its construction in 1566 and again two years later; in 1565 there was despatched to it a cargo of 200 quintals of lead, 150 of arquebus powder, 100 of fine powder, 1,000 earth baskets, and 1,000 shovels with their handles.[4] Before Eulj Ali could mount an attack against it he was called to the aid of the Sultan, who found himself confronted with Spain, the Papacy and Venice joined together in the Christian League. In 1571 this alliance succeeded in swinging the naval balance in the Mediterranean back decisively in favour of the Christian states at the great battle of Lepanto, when the Turks lost some 25,000 men killed and 15,000 slaves freed from their galleys.

The victory of the Christian powers at Lepanto had its repercussions on Tunisia. Don Juan of Austria, the brother of Philip II, took advantage of the supremacy thus gained to occupy Tunis in, 1573. Once again a Hafsid was set up as ruler – Moulay Muhammad, the infant brother of Moulay Hamida. Instead of merely holding La Goulette as Charles V had done, Don Juan left a garrison of some 8,000 men in Tunis itself – although this still fell far short of an occupation of the country as a whole. The following year the Turks counter-attacked. A naval force led by Eulj Ali (who had distinguished himself at Lepanto), and a land force under Sinan Pasha, who had won victories in Yemen – some 230 galleys and 40,000 men – rapidly overcame the Italian-Spanish garrison. In 1574 Tunisia passed under Turkish rule.

The frontiers of the western Mediterranean were now established for two and a half centuries. The Turks had not succeeded in pressing beyond Algeria, and the independence of Morocco was defended by the Saadians, to be followed from 1660 onwards by the Sharifian dynasty. But over Tripoli, Tunis and Algiers Ottoman rule was secure, and these three territories were delimited as Regencies of the Ottoman Empire, with boundaries substantially the same as they have now. Spain was exhausted by bankruptcy, conflict with England, and revolt in the Netherlands, and only retained the *presidios* of Melilla, Mers el-Kebir, and Oran. Fourteen years after Don Juan was ousted from Tunis the Spanish armada against Britain was destroyed and the threat of Spanish domination of Europe, already weakened by the war with Turkey, was ended.

Before this happened Algiers had been developed as a port of major importance, sheltered from the weather and from foreign attack by the constructions designed by Barbarossa. It already served therefore as a base for corsairs. Tunis, although secondary in importance to Algiers, served the same purpose. Both derived revenue from the sale of prizes and the redemption of prisoners and slaves.

From these facts there grew a legendary account of the Barbary coast as being, for some three to four centuries, an uncivilized nest of pirates who preyed on Christian shipping and made the Mediterranean unsafe for peaceful navigation. It is a legend which calls for substantial correction on several counts. Firstly, privateering was different from piracy. Privateers (like Drake and Raleigh) were commissioned to attack enemy shipping in time of war. It was a system of warfare appropriate to an age when great powers were locked in battles that decided the future of Europe – but the sea was still scarcely mastered by frail ships dependent on wind and tide.

(Coming to the relief of Jerba in 1560 Piali Pasha set up a record by sailing from Constantinople to Jerba in twenty days – against the four winter months which the force from Syracuse had taken.) Privateers financed, equipped and fed themselves by private wars which formed part of larger national and religious conflict – making a liberal interpretation of their commission, or relying on the general state of conflict with another power as their justification.

Nor was the practice new: it had existed at least since the time of Homer, and it was universal throughout the Mediterranean. Hence there were rules of the game which were understood by all the participants – which permitted the negotiation of treaties, the sale and redemption of prisoners, and the disposal, through trading, of prizes. Braudel writes:

> Robbers and robbed were not in agreement in advance, as in a perfect *Commedia dell'Arte*, but they were always ready to discuss, then to come to terms. Hence these multiple networks of connivance and complicity (without the complicity of Leghorn and its open door, stolen merchandise would have rotted in the Barbary ports).

A victorious corsair took prisoners and disposed of them. Some remained in prisons for some time; some served as galley slaves; some were sold in the slave markets. Inevitably the fate of Christians captured by the Barbary corsairs excited the emotions of the Europeans. To some extent this was because of the greater clemency which was open under Ottoman rule to those who chose it – a prisoner who accepted Islam could rise high in the service of the Ottomans, as did Eulj Ali, captured originally in Calabria. (No such possibilities were open to Muslims captured by the Christians.) The redemption of captives and slaves therefore took on a religious as well as a humanitarian aspect, and religious orders were established for the purpose – to save Christians from conversion to Islam.

As a result an extremely one-sided picture of the practice of privateering emerged. The Redemptorist fathers had every interest in painting an agonizing picture of the fate of prisoners and slaves in order to raise alms for the continuance of their work; at the same time Christian corsairs who sailed without commissions, or went beyond the commissions they had been given, would claim that they did so under provocation, or to avoid attack. It was in no one's interest to draw attention to the prisons of Malta and Leghorn, the two most important centres for Christian privateering.

Not that the fate of slaves was in any way enviable; it can only be said that self-interest on the part of owners ensured minimal concern for the well-being of the slaves, and that their counterparts in Christian hands were often treated very much worse. They were not branded as Louis XIV's captives were, nor forced to abandon their religion. Although apostasy sometimes brought rewards, it was else-where regarded as dishonourable. The prisons of Tunis were not comfortable, but the Redemptorists were able to rent rooms beside the prisons and say mass constantly in an oratory. Saint Vincent de Paul founded his order to minister to the slaves of Barbary – and they were free to do so.

As the legend of the Barbary pirates developed it was extended to a general condemnation of the government of the states of North Africa – Fez, Tlemcen, Algiers, Tunis and Tripoli. They came to be portrayed as lawless territories where neither person nor property was safe. Yet contemporary accounts show how false such suppositions were. While corsairs ranged the Mediterranean, both England and France were able to develop their trade with the Barbary coast; their citizens lived there and conducted their business; they were secure in the exercise of their religion and benefited from the intervention of their consuls (although in the redemption of slaves, the intervention of a consul was sometimes counterproductive since it had the immediate effect of giving the impression that the slave had wealth behind him).

A single incident serves to show how false reports could lead to accepted fact. In February 1655 Cromwell's admiral, Robert Blake, undertook an expedition to Tunis. The reputation which his action acquired is well represented by the later account of a British naval officer, Edward Blaquière, at the beginning of the nineteenth century. He wrote:

Admiral Blake convinced these people of what a British naval force can perform, when properly conducted. He appeared off the port of Farina; and while his ship battered the town, boats manned and armed destroyed every vessel in the harbour. From thence he went to Tripoly, where the terror of his name obtained the most favourable concessions; and the gallant admiral returning to Tunis, proposed his own terms, which were speedily acceded to.[6]

In fact, however, the origins of Blake's mission do little credit to the cause he represented.[7] The Dey of Tunis had seized a ship named the *Princess* (until a short time before it had been the *Principesa*, under the Spanish flag) in retaliation against action taken by the master of another ship, the *Goodwill*. The master of this ship, Stephen Mitchell, contracted for the conveyance of thirty-two Turks from Tunis to Smyrna. He would not wait for an armed escort, and met some Maltese galleys, to whom he voluntarily surrendered the Turks for a large sum of money after his own crew had plundered their personal possessions. The Dey's first action on receipt of the news was to imprison the British consul; but he then released him to go to Sicily and London to negotiate the release of the Turkish captives. The consul was unsuccessful – the Maltese wanted too much and there was no redress in England – and the Dey then took the traditionally accepted step of seizing another vessel. Blake's purpose was to secure the release of this ship and its crew.

The ships he destroyed at Porto Farina were unmanned and at anchor. They were not difficult to destroy, and Blake justified his uncommissioned act by 'the barbarous carriage of these pirates' – although English merchants were freely trading ashore and two English merchant ships visited the port at the time. But his action did nothing to persuade the Dey to meet his demands. With dignity he informed Blake:

we have our subsistence from the land without needing aught from the sea, neither do we expect anything from sea and therefore he that will negotiate with us let him come ashore and he that will not let him chose.[8]

So Blake got nothing from Tunis; unable to procure water or supplies, he slipped away; he did not go to Tripoli but took on provisions at Algiers. The incident was followed by three years' hostilities between England and Tunis, when by a treaty (Stokes's Treaty) seventy-two captives were redeemed, and the English agreed that 'if any English ship received on board any goods or passengers belonging to the kingdom of Tunis they must both defend them and their goods as far as in their power and not deliver them to the enemy.'

It appears then that Blake's expedition did not originate in reaction to some act of barbarism on the part of the Dey; that it was itself 'punitive' but gained nothing in return, and that Stokes's Treaty included, in the words cited, the safeguarding of the Dey's position. Yet it was this adventure which acquired legendary renown in subsequent years.

The government of Tunisia had not yet become stable – it took a hundred years to do so; but its turbulence did not surpass that of the European states. The state – of which the frontiers were now established – was a Regency of the Ottoman Empire. Initially a Pasha was appointed as governor, supported by a militia force composed at first of Turks and then of Levantine Muslims. This force was made up of 40 sections, each of 100 men and each commanded by a *dey*. In 1590 the deys revolted against their superior officers and elected one of their number as commander of the militia – a position from which successive deys quickly acquired the real authority in the land. However, the Dey depended on an admiral for the command of the fleet and, more important, a Bey who was responsible for the raising of taxes and the government of the tribes. This gave the Beys obvious levers of power, which they exercised. The second Bey, Mourad, was granted the title of pasha and secured the transmission of his post to his son, Hamouda Bey. In 1640 Hamouda, in the tenth year of his rule, had the task of restoring La Goulette after an attack by the Knights of St John from Malta, as well as controlling the tribes in a time of drought. His authority increased accordingly, and his successor, Mourad Bey, ruled as sovereign. But all sovereigns are vulnerable, and in 1702 he was overthrown by a military plot. There followed a period of turmoil while civil conflict was made worse by war with Algeria and Tripoli; but in 1705 a military leader (agha) took power, drove out the Algerians, was proclaimed Bey and suppressed the title of Dey. His name was Husain ibn Ali, and in 1710 he founded the Husainid dynasty, which lasted until the Republic was proclaimed in 1957.

In spite of this upheaval there is much evidence that, by the standards of the time, Tunisia was well governed. Sir Godfrey Fisher quotes the report of Sir Henry Mainwaring, a British privateer who caused some surprise in 1616 by his praise of the administration of Tunis. He wrote:

> In the little observation I could make in my small travels I have noted those Countries best governed where the laws are most severely executed; as for instance in Tunis, where no offence is ever remitted but strictly punished according to their customs and laws. In five months together, when I was coming and going, I never heard of Murder, Robbery or private Quarrel. Nay a Christian, which is more than he can warrant himself in any part of Christendom, may on my knowledge travel 150 miles into the country, though he carry good store of money, and himself alone, and none will molest him.[9]

About fifty years later a Dutchman named Dapper was able to travel freely and safely along the Barbary coast, from Tripoli to Fez. He described the keeping of bees in the hills around Zaghouan, and his account speaks of the rose trees growing just outside Tunis – 'roses and other odiferous plants'.[10] More than a century later Blaquière reported that there were no longer any bees (even though wax was still being exported) but the rose trees were still there. He wrote:

> Many of the opulent natives, and nearly all the European consuls have handsome villas and extensive gardens, which are scattered over the country, from Tunis to a delightful spot called la Marza, close to Cape Carthage, and one of the most luxurious situations

in the kingdom:[11] it is much frequented in summer, when the visitors enjoy the double advantage of exquisite rural recreation and sea-bathing; the number of rose trees cultivated here would surprise an European; for you meet large tracts of ground covered with them, as frequent as turnip fields in England – a promenade in one of these odiferous regions is more easily imagined than described.[12]

The account given by Dapper is confirmed by that of Thomas Shaw, who was chaplain to the English factory at Algiers before being appointed (in 1740) as Principal of St Edmund Hall in Oxford.[13] It was only in the Saharan steppe that he encountered any danger – in that region, he warned travellers, anyone obliged to camp in the open was liable to attack by the Arabs. Elsewhere he travelled with obvious pleasure. He ate 'some of the largest and best mullets that are to be found on the coast of Barbary', caught in the Lake of Tunis (even though he was obliged to cook them himself, because the people were 'utterly ignorant of cookery').

From Tunis Shaw travelled through Cape Bon, where 'the country is extremely fertile and beautiful. Nature displays herself in her gayest forms; rocks, woods, hills, rivers and even the ocean, contribute towards heightening the scene.' He went to Sousse, 'a very considerable city, where the inhabitants carry on a great trade in oil and lemons' and to the 'pleasant village of Monasteer'. From there he continued to Mahdia and then to Sfax – 'a pretty flourishing city, and the inhabitants are industrious, because they do not labour under the same scene of hardships as those in other parts of Barbary'.

Like many travellers today he went inland to Kairouan ('a populous city, and walled round. It is situated in a plain, and carries on a considerable trade'). He enjoyed the pleasures of the desert, in spite of the dangers against which he warned. Of Tozeur he wrote:

The dates of Tozar are most esteemed, and they are exported to Ethiopia, where they are exchanged for black stones, two or three quintals being the price for one. The whole country round this place, is extremely beautiful, for although the sun beams are fierce, yet the cooling plantations make amends.

A striking feature of the travellers' tales from the Barbary coast under Ottoman rule are the comments made on the 'civility' of the Tunisians. Thomas Shaw reported that:

> The Tunisians are the most civilised people who inhabit the coast of the Mediterranean; for instead of plundering their neighbours, they addict themselves to trade and commerce, which induces them to cultivate the friendship of the Christians. This is, undoubtedly, much to their honour; for by living honestly, they acquire respect even by those who do not chuse to follow their example.

A century later another English writer, G. A. Jackson (who drew on the account of Thomas MacGill and others), wrote in terms of greater condescension, but to the same effect. He reported:

> But though we have said that the Tunisians greatly resemble the Algerines, they are agreeably distinguished from them by their superior politeness and civilization, and by their being exempted from that pride, insolence, and barbarity, for which the natives of this coast are justly stigmatized. They are affable in their manners, friendly and obliging to strangers, and faithful to their compacts. The extension of commerce, the improvement of manufactures, and the friendships they have formed with the European powers, have no doubt contributed to this happy effect on their minds; . . .
>
> Jealousy, which appears to be endemial in Barbary, prevails less at Tunis than perhaps in any other state, which we have described in this part of the globe. . . .
>
> The taverns are under much better regulations than those in the neighbouring countries; and even a Turk, who is guilty of intoxication, and behaves insolently, may be deprived of his turban until he has made satisfaction.[14]

The condescension of Jackson was surpassed by the transparent prejudice of Blaquière, whose admiration for Admiral Blake has already been noted. Blaquière believed the country to be blinded by superstition and distinguished by its savage ferocity; and he honestly admits his surprise to find that 'besides the Jewish synagogues, Greek and Roman Catholic chapels are established in the centre of the town.' Similarly he starts from the presupposition that 'to look for virtue or principle in a Barbary chief, would be an idle task', and it is not surprising therefore that he should be puzzled that the Bey had ruled so successfully for so long. Yet the picture he draws is of a hardworking ruler – albeit one who 'was never known to refuse a present from any of his suitors, and has even, in many instances, accepted a bribe from both parties.' He describes the Bey's government thus:

> His attention to public business is unwearied and really astonishing; very little of his time is devoted to sleep. He never associates with his women, so that the greater part of the day is passed, either in the divan, or hall of justice, which opens every morning, the sabbath excepted (Friday) at eight o'clock, and continues open till twelve, when he retires to dinner; after which, a short time is devoted to sleep, and the remainder of the afternoon to various arrangements in the state. The consuls of foreign nations are generally received at seven in the morning, in the hall of audience. . . .
>
> The Bey is supreme magistrate and judge in his own dominions; he passes a considerable part of each day in the hall of justice, and constant habits of observation have made him such a physiognomist, that where self-interest does not interfere, his judgement has seldom been known to err. . . .
>
> Without the intervention of lawyers or attorneys, this Bey's decision is as quick in delivery as in execution . . . and the aggrieved have, at least, the satisfaction of immediate reparation, while this manner of executing the law produces a most powerful sensation on the people.[15]

From these accounts a clear picture of a relatively static society emerges. Nominally under Ottoman rule, Tunisia was in practice independent of the Turks, although it did not have the characteristics of a nation state. Government was in the hands of the Bey and his advisers, who were drawn from the Mameluke class – coming from almost anywhere round the shores of the Mediterranean or the borders of Turkey and making a career in the service of the Sultan and his nominal regents. The trade of the seaports – especially Tunis – was very largely in the hands of Jews and of foreigners. The latter enjoyed the protection of their consuls, and (in accordance with the normal capitulation treaties signed originally with the Turkish government) came under their jurisdiction even though they lived in the territory of the Regency.

Privateering and the commerce associated with it formed a declining industry, and disappeared altogether after the Napoleonic wars. Tunisia continued to manufacture and to trade – it exported woollen covers, olive oil, lemons, wheat and Morocco leather, as well as dates, hides, wax and soap. It was known for the manu-facture of the *chechia* or skull cap, made in Tunis and dyed red in dye mixed with the waters of Zaghouan. Jackson, following MacGill, reports that

> the manufacture of caps in Tunis is upon an establishment which would do no discredit to an European country, and is much superior to what could have been expected, under such a govern-ment, and in such a state of society as that of Tunis.[16]

But while traditional agriculture and crafts kept the society alive, they did not provide for its growth. The art of government remained at a rudimentary level and varied widely according to the talents and character of the ruling Bey. Taxation often succeeded in keeping the people poor without enriching the government. Defence forces were minimal; roads were not built.

Given the history of Tunisia in earlier centuries it is inconceivable that this state of affairs could continue for ever. Repeatedly the country had suffered invasion, its fate closely linked to that of a dominant power in the Mediterranean or the Middle East – Phoen-icia, Rome, Islam, Spain or Turkey. In the nineteenth century it was brought yet closer to Europe, as ships ceased to be at the mercy of wind and tide and could navigate in a straight line across the Mediterranean at the time of their choosing.

In Europe the ideas and the organization of the nation state grew rapidly, accelerated by the wars of the French Revolution and Napoleon. As this happened the traders and consuls who for centuries had lived content under the regime of the capitulations became the agents and the excuse for imperial expansion. With perception born of national jealousy Blaquière observed:

> The number of French subjects in the Regency, together with the facility with which his Highness admits others, may, on some future day, interfere very materially with his interests, if they do not already.[17]

Tunisia had always been open to the world and the development of Europe inspired its ruling class to emulation. But modernization is a disruptive force; and the modernizers had to compete with a Europe engaged in the pursuit of power, prestige and profit. It was, in the first instance, an unequal contest.

6   French occupation

THE STABILITY and ordered succession of the Husainid dynasty was an achievement in itself. Before the middle of the nineteenth century this stability began to break down, until a new order was established in 1881 with the occupation of Tunisia by France and the establish‑ ment of the French protectorate. The Tunisian governing class – the Bey and his advisers – sought to modernize their own society. Few of these men were born in Tunisia; they belonged to a Mameluke class – men who had entered the service of Ottoman rulers as slaves and then worked their way to high office. They were familiar with the series of reforms – the Tanzimat – which had begun in Turkey in 1826, and they were sensitive to the modern efficiency of European society.

When they sought to change their own environment – to modernize the state and improve their own position as a ruling class – they did not do so in a vacuum. The rise of European power and technology acquired unprecedented momentum in the indus‑ trial age which followed the French Revolution. The growth of industry and banking meant that money could be mobilized in Europe, seeking a quick return on investment in developing countries. As industry was allied to the efficiency of the European nation‑state the frontiers of Europe extended outwards. European powers acquired overseas interests, and entered into rivalry with each other far beyond their own frontiers. Increasingly they became persuaded that the defence of their strategic, political and economic interests – as well as the struggle for supremacy in Europe – required the extension of political rule overseas. As a result an unstable relationship was established between Europe and the undeveloped areas of the world, of which Tunisia formed part.

The new wave of European expansion first reached North Africa when French troops disembarked in Algeria in May 1830. The causes of this decisive action – which started a long train of events, eventually leading more than a hundred years later to the re-establishment of de Gaulle's government in France – appear trivial in retrospect. Before the occupation the French position at Algiers was already strong, French interests were not threatened, and there was no obvious reason to embark on a lengthy colonial war to establish political control.

The occupation arose from a squalid dispute in which the French government was engaged with two Algerian Jews, who had supplied France with large quantities of wheat, saving the *midi* from famine under the Directorate – and who had never been paid. In the course of negotiations the Bey of Algiers struck the French consul with his fan. He can hardly have realized that he was providing the pretext for military intervention. The more fund-amental motive of the government of Charles X was to re-establish the position of France amongst the powers of Europe, and to try to regain authority within France.

The occupation of Algeria did not immediately create any danger for Tunisia. Indeed, the Bey welcomed it as a diminution of the traditional threat from the east. The French government maintained its interests in Tunisia, for their own sake and as a safeguard to Algeria. But these interests in Tunisia were not threatened and there was no wish to establish an exclusive trading monopoly. A bishop under French patronage, Monsignor Sutter, ministered, from 1843, to the needs of Catholics in conditions of wide religious tolerance and without attempting any missionary activity amongst Muslims. The Bey accepted French protection vis-à-vis the Turkish government; but as the pressure from the latter was minimal, so was the degree of protection against it.

Meanwhile modernizing reforms were pressed forward. Ahmed Bey (who ruled from 1837 to 1855) was inordinately impressed by the armies of France and Egypt – the former of which had conquered

Algeria and the latter, under Mehemet Ali, ranged far into Syria and Arabia. He persuaded the French to send a military mission and constructed a vast if ephemeral army. To supply it he established a textile factory (worked by English weavers) and a leather works. With the outbreak of the Crimean war, in which both France and Turkey were engaged as allies against Russia, a sad contingent of Tunisian troops was sent to Constantinople – where no one had any use for them and they suffered from the same ravages of illness which decimated armies from countries more developed than their own.

At its best the modernization of Tunisia in the conditions of the mid-nineteenth century would have been disruptive and threatened the survival of a weak political framework. Worse, the grandeur and the opulence to be found in Europe held a fascination for some Tunisians, who were willing to borrow money in the pursuit of their personal fortune.

Such money was at first readily available. The development of banking in Europe permitted the emergence of a group of financiers capable of mobilizing money and lending it outside Europe at high rates of interest, and with terms which ensured their own reward whether or not interest or capital payments were ever made. When Ahmed Bey sought to emulate the glories of Versailles by building a great palace at Mohammedia, international lenders were unlikely to warn him that Versailles had been the prelude to 1789; but the fact was that extravagance and borrowing could only be met, as earlier they had been in France, by taxing the poor, until the poor revolted.

At the same time the interests of the European powers in Tunisia changed. They did so in part in response to the growing instability of Tunisian society and the consequent threat to their own interests. A stronger motive was the growth of rivalry between them, led by their consuls and religious leaders on the spot. The dominant position of France in Tunisia was challenged first by Richard Wood, a British consul of exceptional energy and determination, and later by Licurgo Maccio, consul of a newly united Italy. When the French at last decided to occupy Tunisia they did so in order to preserve the prestige and position of France as a great power.

The monuments to the turbulent period which preceded French occupation are still prominent in the region of Tunis. To the south-west the windy ruins of Ahmed Bey's palace stand within sight of the old Roman aqueduct bringing water from Zaghouan – which was repaired at great expense in the nineteenth century only to cause further discontent when the townspeople of Tunis discovered they had to pay for the water and the villagers found the aqueduct too well guarded for them to siphon it off. Across the Lake of Tunis runs the railway to La Goulette and La Marsa – the TGM. It was built by an English company under the persuasion of the British consul, Richard Wood, who was intent on spreading British influence throughout the Regency; when the railway proved un-profitable it was sold at a price immensely inflated by competition between the French and Italians – a battle which the Italians won, thereby pushing the French government a step nearer to occupation and eventual elimination of Italian influence. While the Moham-media is in ruins, the villa of the Erlanger family, at Sidi bou Said, still testifies to the fortune which could be made in moneylending in an underdeveloped country.

The greatest of the Tunisian modernizers was Khair al-Din Pasha – a Circassian, born in the Caucasus and taken to Istanbul, from where he was brought into the service of Ahmed Bey as a 'slave' or Mameluke. He was educated in French as well as Arabic, entered the army, and was then sent to Paris to defend the interests of the Tunisian government in a legal case against a former minister. The years he spent there, at the beginning of the second empire, had a deep formative influence on him. On his return to Tunisia he was associated with the major developments of the next twenty years. He became Minister of Marine and so was in a position to press the Bey to introduce political reform. Pressure from within Tunis was supported by that of the great powers, who urged the Bey to intro-duce measures similar to those adopted by the Turkish government after the Crimean war. The precipitating factor in this situation was a sudden outburst of religious intolerance. In 1857 a Jewish carter was summarily executed, after trial in a Muslim court. Vigorous protest was now added to pressure, and Mohammed Bey announced his intention of granting a constitution. Khair al-Din took part in its drafting, and became president of the Council it established.

But the new Constitution, introduced in 1861, solved no problems. It severely circumscribed the powers of the Bey, who became a constitutional sovereign; but it established a council which could only be drawn from a small group of notables. Many of them shared Khair al-Din's Mameluke origins, but few his interest in reform. Above all it did not limit the power of Khair al-Din's rival who had already been prime minister for twenty-four years and was to remain for a further twelve – Mustapha Khaznadar, whose daughter Khair al-Din had married.

Mustapha Khaznadar had been born Georges Kalkias Stravelakis and his father had been murdered during the massacre of Chios in 1821. Georges and his brother were taken to Constantinople, sold to Tunis, and converted to Islam. Mustapha grew up as the playmate of Ahmed Bey and then ruled at his side (after they had arranged the strangling of Mustapha's rival). He survived the succession of Mohamed (1857) and Mohamed Sadok (1859), and held power while the latter enjoyed a life of debauchery. But in the conduct of Tunisian affairs he lived from one daily expedient to another, and had the single long-term policy of enriching himself and providing for his own security.[1] Entrenched in power, he was able to secure the removal of Khair al-Din in 1862 and reigned supreme until foreign pressure and domestic intrigue effected the return of Khair al-Din in 1873.

The damage which Mustapha Khaznadar could do was immense, in a country which was open to any and every form of public works, and which attracted foreign money looking for a quick profit. Reforms which were desirable in themselves – such as reconstruction of the army – easily proved disproportionately expensive; public works were undertaken without regard to cost – whether the building of the four-kilometre road from Tunis to the Bardo, or the reconstruction of the aqueduct for twelve million francs. The availability of foreign credit added to the public debt and in consequence to the taxation necessary to service it. Private bankers like Erlanger made no attempt to control or supervise the use of loans they made;

while a consul like Richard Wood sought to establish his own patronage over foreign lending rather than exercise financial discipline.

Extravagance and innovation alike spread discontent. Increased spending led to increased taxes. Judicial reform, admirable on paper, in practice removed justice further from the beduin into the towns and increased the power of the Mameluke class at the expense of the local notables. In Tunisia as elsewhere the spread of the telegraph was seen as a threat by the nomadic tribes. In the spring of 1864 revolt spread across the country – unorganized, aiming at pillage rather than power but spreading disorder and insecurity everywhere except in major towns. In spite of attempted reform the army remained weak and ineffective; but by the autumn the revolt had worn itself out, broken by small-scale rivalries and bribery, to be followed by harsh repression – and the suspension of the constitution.

During the insurrection Britain, France and Turkey had sent warships to the coast of Tunis; but none of the great powers wanted to intervene except to protect their own nationals and keep the others out; the exhaustion of the rebellion made it unnecessary for them to do so. Five years later their intervention took another form. Fresh loans were followed by renewed bankruptcy, and in 1869 the Bey had no choice but to accept the establishment of an international commission in control of Tunisian finances, with the dominant position held by a French inspector. The establishment of the commission brought the renewed ascendancy of Khair al-Din, first as the Tunisian member of the Commission and then as prime minister. His initial appointment was due to Khaznadar – who did not foresee that the close cooperation between Khair al-Din and the French inspector, Villet, would reveal accumulating evidence of his maladministration and embezzlement, or that the French government would mount increasing pressure to secure his removal.

Appointed prime minister in 1873, Khair al-Din made no attempt to restore constitutional government. He tried rather to modernize Tunisia by administrative reform and by training a class of incorruptible and sound government servants, educated in a

Muslim tradition. He extended the financial reform (of which he and Villet had already laid the foundation) by controlling public expenditure, removing corrupt administrators and improving debt collection. He tried to promote agricultural reform and carried out municipal improvement in Tunis – paving and draining roads, restoring public buildings.

Khair al-Din also promoted the extension and improvement of schools throughout Tunisia, reformed teaching at the Zitouna mosque, and established a public library. Most important innovation of all, he founded Sadiki College, a new school whose purpose was to train civil servants and members of the liberal professions. A major part in the curriculum was given to traditional Islamic studies, led by teachers from the Mosque; but provision was made also for the teaching of French and Italian, mathematics and science. The endowment of the College was provided from the sequestrated estates of Mustapha Khaznadar.

In addition Khair al-Din sought to maintain the independence of Tunisia from the great powers. Before becoming prime minister he had travelled to Constantinople, as he had already done on two previous occasions, to persuade the Sultan of Turkey to reaffirm his sovereignty over an autonomous Tunisia – and thus create a counter-balance to French influence. On this occasion he succeeded in getting the *firman* he sought. But it proved inadequate defence against French influence, led by a consul determined to press French interests against those of Britain and Italy. Nor did Khair al-Din succeed in establishing a political base in domestic politics from which to resist the counter pressures his reforms and his haughty bearing were bound to create. In 1877 he was forced from office. He returned to Constantinople where, briefly, he repeated his Tunisian experience as grand vizir to the young Abdul Hamid – to be dismissed in 1879 and die in retirement ten years later.

The sum of Khair al-Din's career may appear to be one of failure. His attempt to restore Tunisian independence was shortly followed by French occupation, his administrative reforms ran into the ground. But two permanent achievements outweigh the frustra-tions of his career. He was a precursor of modern Arab political thought. He wrote a political essay which was published first in Tunis in 1867 and then in Constantinople and Paris. In this work he urged the restoration of the Islamic community to its former strength, by drawing from Europe its institutions – responsible ministers, parliaments, a free press and the diffusion of knowledge. It was these institutions, he argued, which gave Europe its vigour and were responsible for its success. Islamic society, by adapting them to its needs, could regain its former greatness.[2]

To this theoretical contribution Khair al-Din added the establishment of Sadiki College. Initially it formed the cadres, not of a Tunisian state (as Khair al-Din intended), but of a nationalist movement. Only eighty years later did it become the training ground for the servants of an independent Tunisia.

The fall of Khair al-Din put an end to any immediate prospect of reform in Tunisia. But it was not this so much as events in the international sphere which now moved France towards the occupation of the country. In 1875 nationalist revolts in the Balkans opened a fresh crisis in the eastern Mediterranean, provoked a war between Russia and Turkey and nearly brought the armed intervention of Britain and France, renewing the conflict of the Crimean war. To safeguard British interests and provide a *place d'armes* against the renewal of a similar eastern crisis Disraeli's government acquired the island of Cyprus (still under the nominal sovereignty of Turkey). Their action meant a change in the Mediterranean balance of power, for which they expected to have to make some concession to France; the concession they proposed was that France should feel free to occupy Tunisia. Equally important, the British proposal had the support of Bismarck, anxious to turn French attention away from Alsace-Lorraine and initiate an improvement in Franco-German relations.

The action of the British government meant the abandonment of a policy which their consul in Tunis had pursued and urged on his masters for twenty years. Richard Wood was born in Constantinople and had begun his career there at the time when Palmerston was working against French influence in the eastern Mediterranean. In 1841 he went as consul to Damascus. Appointed to Tunis in

1856 he made it his business to combat the French position and extend his own, and therefore British influence. The leading French authority on the subject has said of him:

> His favourite weapons were ruse and pretence, his normal methods negotiations hatched in great secrecy, the results of which he only unveiled at the last moment. Flattering, and indeed cunning, he dissembled his action behind a modest exterior and pushed understudies into the foreground, pretending to play only a secondary role.[3]

In more prosaic terms, his means of action were to insist (on behalf of the British government) on the fact of Turkish sovereignty (since British influence was strong in Constantinople), to diminish the French position, to gain the alliance of Mustapha Khaznadar, and to promote British economic interests in Tunisia as a lever with which to claim and to exercise political rights. He set himself a thankless task. His enthusiasm for the development of economic enterprise was not shared by British companies who sought profitable investment rather than political levers (as the experience of the Tunis–Goulette railway showed). His government either subordinated Tunisian questions to the need for good relations with France or, if it quarrelled with France, did so on more central issues nearer to home ground. After the Congress of Berlin and the offer to France, Richard Wood was retired and died in obscurity, his place taken by Thomas Reade, who gave no trouble to the French.

The withdrawal of British pressure on the French in Tunis might possibly have restored the position to that of an earlier period, when French influence was predominant and unchallenged, without any need for the expense and complication of occupation. But as the British withdrew so the Italians took on a more aggressive role. The leverage which they could exercise was based on a rapidly increasing Italian population, Catholic missions and schools, and the acquisition of economic interests. They were represented by an active and energetic consul in Licurgo Maccio, who was given support by his own government in a way Wood had never been. Indeed the Italian government believed that it too had been encouraged by Bismarck to annexe Tunisia – as well as Tripoli, which the British, for their part, regarded as adequate compensation for this newcomer to the game of European power politics.

But although Italy held some levers in Tunisia, it plied these levers from a position of weakness. Britain was always in a position to embarrass France in other areas of world politics, or, in the last resort, to use its naval power to back up its position in Tunis. The Italians lacked the same resources. The more they pressed an advantage in Tunisia therefore – as they did when the Italian government provided the resources to outbid the French in the purchase of the Tunis–Goulette railway – the more likely were the French to respond by an occupation which would secure their position for good.

This was the more so since French interests in North Africa were pressed by agents at least as vigorous as Wood and Maccio. In 1874 the French government had sent Theodore Roustan, one of its best political agents, to be Consul and Chargé d'affaires at Tunis. He too had pursued his early career in the east – in Beirut, Cairo and Alexandria. In the same way that Wood had done he pressed for the development of Tunisia by French enterprises – in the building of a port, of railways and a telegraph. After 1878 battle was joined with the Italians at every level. Rival claims to be the legal purchaser of the TGM railway were fought out in the High Court in London; negotiations for the purchase of Khair al-Din's estate at Enfida by the Société marseillaise were fought by a Jew of British citizenship (born in Gibraltar) with the backing of the Italians, taking advant-age of the idiosyncrasies of Muslim law. It was a personal as well as a political battle – the careers of Roustan and Maccio had run parallel, and they were renewing a contest begun thirteen years previously in Cairo.

But Roustan was not the only Frenchman pressing French interests. In 1867 one of the great Christian empire-builders of the nineteenth century, Lavigerie, had been appointed Archbishop of Algiers. He was a man of immense energy, wide-ranging vision, occupying a post of key importance in the politics of the period.

He was dedicated to the spread of French Catholic interests in Africa and the Near East. (In common with the other principal characters of the story he had also spent part of his early career in Syria before becoming Bishop of Nancy.)

For Lavigerie North Africa was the home of the early Christian church. It had nurtured Tertullian and Augustine and safeguarded the Christian religion when it was challenged by paganism in Rome. It was the land of the martyrdom of Saint Louis, whose crusade Lavigerie would willingly renew in the changed conditions of his century. Taking up his diocese in May 1867 he had conceived his mission and that of his flock in these terms:

> To make the land of Algeria the cradle of a great, generous Christian nation, of another France in a word . . . to link North Africa and Central Africa to the life of the Christian people, this is part of the design of God, the hopes of *la patrie* and of the Church, your providential destiny.

The following year he established the order of the White Fathers, who were to contribute much to the welfare and scholarship of North Africa.

For twenty-five years Lavigerie held a pivotal place. As France entered on the secularizing reforms of the Third Republic the legend of Christian North Africa acquired increasing force amongst Catholics and on the Right. But although the French Republican government curtailed the power of the Church in France, it supported Lavigerie in the work which he and his missions did to extend French influence overseas. The government presented him for the cardinalcy in 1881. Deeply patriotic, he sought an end to the conflict between the church and the republic, and later became Leo XIII's agent in preparing the way for papal acceptance of the republican form of government in France. His personal ambition fitted ideally into French interests – in 1880 he secured the creation of four apostolic vicariates under French priests, so that 'from the frontiers of Algeria to those of the English and Dutch colonies of the Cape of Good Hope the whole interior of Africa is henceforth placed, from the religious point of view, under French authority.'[4]

He succeeded Sutter as Vicar Apostolic in Tunis and then, in 1884, was created Archbishop of Carthage as well as Algiers. As he pointed out to the French government, the protectorate alone would be insufficient to safeguard French interests against the Italians unless supreme religious authority were given to a French archbishop.

Meanwhile in the decisive years after the Congress of Berlin Lavigerie was already active in extending French influence. The French consul was proving victorious over his English and Italian rivals; but the European population of Tunis included a high proportion of Maltese and Italians. As Catholics they were receptive to the leadership of Lavigerie, who won their allegiance. As a Frenchman he had the backing of his government; as a Catholic Archbishop he had the support of the Pope. The Vatican in any case had no reason to support Italian political influence in Tunisia, since its relations with the Italian government were worse than those with France.

But whatever the activities of Frenchmen in North Africa, the occupation of Tunisia could only be decided by the government in Paris. There opposition to such a forward movement was strong. There were too many internal problems to be taken into account, electoral fortunes to be considered, the difficulty of obtaining credits to be thought of. But in the spring of 1881 the pressures on the government mounted steadily, kept up by the insistence of the political director of the foreign office, in close touch with Roustan in Tunis. The turning point came when Gambetta, who was President of the Chamber of Deputies, was persuaded that the future of France as a great power depended on the occupation of Tunisia, both as a safeguard of French interests and as an assertion of French power.

It remained to determine the occasion for intervention. The opportunity soon presented itself in an insurrection of the Khroumir tribes on the Algerian frontier. French troops entered Tunisia from Algeria. They met no resistance from the Tunisians. In May 1881 the Bey signed an agreement with the French government which came to be known as the Treaty of Bardo, whereby France was given the right to military occupation and control over foreign affairs and finance. Two years later a further treaty, signed at La Marsa in June 1883, completed the establishment of the French protectorate.

Meanwhile the Treaty of Bardo had encountered strident opposition within France. Left-wing nationalists mounted an attack on the financial interests which had benefited from occupation, and forced the resignation of Roustan on the grounds that he had engineered the occupation for his own advantage. In reply those who supported the occupation did so, as is often the case in the immediate aftermath of imperial expansion, by stressing the limited nature of the protectorate, designed, they said, to rehabilitate Tunisia without any attempt to impose French ways on the Muslims.

But at the same time the natural reflexes of those engaged in an imperialist enterprise were already evident. The foreign office sent J. J. Jusserand (who later became Ambassador to the United States) to investigate the charges brought against Roustan, and he wrote a general report on Tunisia. In the opening paragraph of his note on education he wrote:

> We have at the moment no better means of assimilating to us the Arabs of Tunisia, as far as that is possible, than by teaching them our language. . . . We cannot count on religion to achieve this assimilation; they will never be converted to Christianity; but to the extent that they learn our idiom a host of European ideas will be revealed to them, as experience has shown.[5]

Up to a point Jusserand's words were prophetic. French education did reveal European ideas to the élite who were fortunate enough to have such education; but the result was that they aspired to independence, not assimilation.

Over the ensuing years there were two easily predictable developments which rapidly led to Frenchmen seeing the French position in Tunisia not as a means of keeping other European powers out and protecting (for politics and profit) their economic interests, but as something vital for the integrity of France itself. The first was the growth and development of the institutions of French government, and the second the colonization of the country by Frenchmen.

As early as 1886 another representative of the French government visiting Tunisia, J. L. de Lanessan, discussed the 'speculative' nature of land purchase in Tunisia, and in two short pages of his report was able to reach the conclusion that the government should do everything possible to maintain the speed of this 'civilizing progress'.[6] The idea of Tunisia as a Muslim country whose inhabitants could not be converted began to take second place. Paul Cambon, the first ministerresident, wrote a history of Tunisia beginning in the year 1270 – the year of St Louis's crusade; the great cathedral of Carthage was built near the site of St Louis's tomb; a statue of Lavigerie was erected at the entrance to the Arab town of Tunis, and a Christian ecumenical congress was held in Tunis in 1931. A major naval base was constructed at Bizerte.

The practical arguments and the competition of power politics which had led to the establishment of the protectorate were now clothed with an ideology of imperialism: the need for a French presence, the interests and security of France, the civilizing mission of France – indeed the importance of the French 'protectorate' to the welfare of Tunisia itself.

16–17 Métameur: ruined *ghorfas* (*above*). In the past Tunisians, like all people facing the challenge of a harsh natural environment, have constructed shelters for themselves from materials closest to hand, whether branches and skins, natural clay or Roman building stones. But the climate, exacting and devastating as it may be in the steppe and the desert, attracts tourists to the beaches, where they may live in the elegant comfort of modern hotels (*right*), and provide revenue and foreign currency for economic development.

18 The end of the afternoon in Tunisian villages brings relief from the heat. Women and children go to draw water (*above*), either in the centre of the village or at some distance to the nearest well or tap, while men congregate in the cafés. For both it is a social occasion of major importance.

19 The island of Jerba shelters the two important but diminishing Jewish communities of Hara Kebira and Hara Srira, the former with its synagogue (called 'the Marvellous'). Although the tradition of the synagogue goes back to 600 BC, the present buildings date only from 1920. They provide both a religious sanctuary and a meeting-place for the reading and commenting of the Scriptures (*left*).

20 The coast of Jerba gives hospitality to tourists. But the island
continues to shelter the descendants of the Kharijites, Berber is spoken,
and Jerbians have emigrated to dominate the small commerce of Tunisia.

21 The harshness of the Tunisian climate comes not only from the heat but from the cold of the desert night and the biting winds of the steppe. Hedges of cactus (prickly pear) and trees are supplemented by hurdles of bamboo to provide shelter for nursery plants (*above*).

22 Fishermen leave Mahdia (*below*). Their methods are traditional, their means have been modernized – multiple electric lights in the stern of their boats attract the fish to their nets. When these are brought ashore they no longer have to be sold on the quayside but are marketed through the National Fishing Office.

23 Traditionally olive trees have been grown in small allotments, tended more or less well, often allowed to grow too old. Wasteful where rainfall is adequate, cultivation of this sort is impossible further south, around Sfax. Instead, vast estates of olive trees were planted (*above*), widely spread and carefully tended so that the roots spread and nourish themselves from the dew.

24–26 Tunisia has few natural resources – although its neighbours, Algeria and Libya, are rich in oil and natural gas. Salt is shown (*above*) after being dried in pans beside the sea, south of Monastir. Lead is mined around Béja and smelted into ingots (*left*). Iron-ore is found near the Algerian frontier, and phosphates mined in quantity. *Right:* Traditional crafts constitute an added resource and are supported and promoted by the National Artisanate Office. Their products are exported, and meanwhile employment is provided and distinctive regional designs, like that of Gafsa shown here, are preserved.

27 President Bourguiba and his wife are welcomed by the crowds in Kairouan. Madame Wassila Bourguiba (the President's second wife, whom he married in 1955) has taken a leading part in the National Union of Tunisian Women and provides an example of the new role accorded to women in modern Tunisia.

7 Tunisian nationalism

TUNISIA DID NOT THEREBY BECOME FRENCH. On the contrary, Tunisian nationalism took shape in response to French rule.
Tunisian thought about the nature, structure and purpose of government was influenced by contact with France; the ideals of self-
government, which would surely have emerged anyway, took their
particular form from contact with France; the ideology of Tunisia
as part of France evoked counter-feelings of the independent nature
of a Tunisian community.

From the first the French occupation had to come to terms with a
complicated system of Islamic land ownership. This was necessary
even for the limited purposes of the establishment of military camps,
far more so with the growth of colonization. Relatively little Tunisian
land was owned privately – it belonged to the personal domain of
the Bey, or to rich families, many of them of Turkish origin, or in
small part to peasants in the Sahel. Some was tribal land, belonging
collectively to the nomad tribes of the south. The major part of the
most useful land was owned under a system of mainmort and known
as *habous* land. The profit from the land went to a religious foundation; but in a large number of cases it was to do so only when the
descendants of the man who had originally left the land as *habous*
had died out. There were thus public *habous* under the administration of a member of the religious leadership of the country; private
habous which were also inalienable but the revenue from which still
went to private persons; and a small third category from which
private persons drew the excess over a guaranteed sum available for
pious works. To complicate matters further it was customary for the

owners of private land (and for tribal owners) to have a *habous* arrangement in reserve as a safeguard against possible expropriation.

One of the first actions of the French protectorate was to establish a legal framework for the acquisition of land in a European manner. It did so by an Act of 1885 which was based on the Torrens Act, passed for similar purposes in different conditions in Australia. It was the first in a series of legislative acts which made possible the private acquisition of land. The problem of mainmort was got round and eventually pushed aside by replacing the yearly payment by a single lump payment.

The application of this legislation was of major importance in Tunisian development. Its immediate practical effect was to make colonization possible; it had a far deeper impact on society. The administration of the 1885 Act was put in the hands of mixed tribunals, so that French and Tunisians sat side by side deciding claims to ownership. They came from very different backgrounds and represented different systems of law. Their association provided fresh insight and fresh knowledge, which contributed on the one side to an understanding of European law and on the other to an awareness of Islamic civilization. More important for the future, it set an example of the acquisition of right by legal means which could be extended to the political sphere and contribute to the building of a nationalist movement. Later it also provided a legal framework in which young Tunisians could defend the interests of the underprivileged in their society, defending in a court of law the rights and status of sharecroppers and the like, developing thereby a social philosophy intertwined with the demand for political rights. Bourguiba's early career was spent in this way.

Land was bought in part by private purchasers, in part by the French government, which could then resell it and so encourage colonization. At the time of the occupation the number of French men in Tunisia was very small: French influence was essentially political – following from proximity to France and contiguity with Algeria – and economic. Of an estimated population of one and a half millions there were less than twenty thousand Europeans and of these only 708 were French – the mass were some 11,000 Italians and 7,000 Maltese. By 1946 there were a quarter of a million Europeans, and of these the French accounted for nearly 150,000, and the Italians 85,000, while the Maltese had remained approxi-mately constant. There was a considerable Jewish population – impossible to count accurately, since some were numbered as 'Europeans' in the French census, but probably in the region of 75,000.

The purchase of land tended to be on a large scale, and the French settlement was characterized by large colonial estates. Colonization on a small scale never occurred in spite of French efforts – a fact which later made the transition to independence and Tunisian ownership much easier. The Europeans grew wheat, increasing the production of soft wheat, and they introduced the production of hay. Vineyards, as one would expect, were owned almost entirely by Europeans and were concentrated in the hands of few individuals or companies. The European part in the growth of olive trees remained relatively small (some 15–20 per cent of the total). It too was dominated by large companies, and represented a disproportionately high part of the output of oil since the large European estates were better placed geographically or used better methods of production.

European settlers could and did look with pride as the second generation of colonization bore fruit, contrasting the well-arranged and accurately aligned estates which they had created with the apparent disorder of Arab lands. They could believe that they had brought the land to life, and revel in the pleasures of imperialism – a sense of enterprise and pioneering spirit which those at home lacked, warmed by sunshine and a multiplicity of servants.

From the Tunisian point of view the appearance was quite different. True, Tunisians remained landowners; there were many middle-class farmers who had taken advantage of the new law to purchase land; the major part of olive-oil production remained in their hands; in the oases the production of dates was scarcely affected by colonization. Nonetheless as Jacques Berque has shown in his perceptive analysis, a fundamental instability existed between the settlers' estates and the Arab lands round about. The estates enjoyed all the advantages of the operation of the law and the input of capital and technology, and the result of this was to create islands of prosperity, which did little to enrich the country as a whole, and which supported a minimum number of workers – in contrast to the growing population of underemployed outside the European estates. It is scarcely surprising therefore that, as Berque has written:

> The most provocative symbol of the colonial epoch in the Maghreb is that of the tiled farmhouse, a cheerful dwelling standing amid vineyards. It aroused the most violent, and violently opposed, reactions from Frenchmen and the people of the Maghreb. The fact that it was surrounded by more significant forces matters little; it implied all the rest. Banks, military camps, factories and schools may have played at least as important a part, but none made so deep an impression on everyone's feelings as this French farmstead, this heraldic emblem on African soil.[1]

Later, the experience of colonial rule provided a warning for independent Tunisia – The European estates had gone far in increasing productivity in their own sector, and this must be an objective of any programme of economic growth; but it does not by itself solve social problems in a country with wide diversities of climate and fertility.

Meanwhile the governmental structure of Tunisia continued to be based on the fiction of a protectorate. The most important change in government was the extension of its scope – and this was necessarily in French hands. The Bey retained nominal sovereignty; but real authority rested with the French Resident-General, under the direction of the French foreign office. There was a Tunisian prime minister and sometimes a 'minister of the pen', and the traditional areas of Tunisian government came under their jurisdiction. These included the administration of Muslim law by Islamic judges, the administration of the *habous*, Muslim education and the religious brotherhoods. Even this sphere of government did not escape French supervision, exercised by a 'delegate'; but the protectorate avoided interference with the personal law of Islam or with the exercise of religion. Secularization had to wait for independence.

The Resident-General exercised legislative authority – he pre-

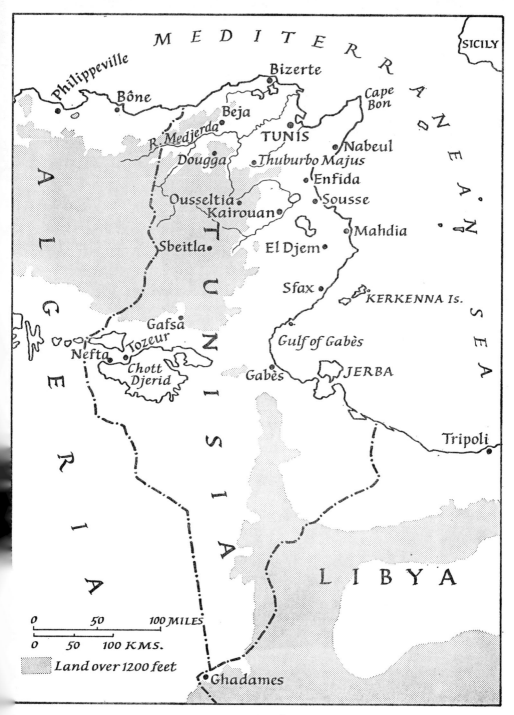

Tunisia today

pared Beylical decrees, promulgated and enforced them. The government was divided into departments, including finance, public works, economic affairs, public instruction – each headed by a 'directeur'. These directors, together with the Tunisian ministers, the army and navy commanders (French) and the Resident-General formed a Council of Ministers and heads of services.

The decisive power of the Resident-General was supplemented by a primitive system of representation, of a consultative and advisory sort. In 1896 a consultative conference was established, and this was enlarged in 1907 to include sixteen Tunisian members appointed by the Resident-General (the French members being elected). In 1922 a Grand Council was created, consisting of two sections, one French and the other Tunisian. The system of representation was devised to ensure the preponderance of propertied interests even in the French section, and by a complex system of indirect election in the Tunisian section. The government was not responsible to the Council, nor did the latter hold any final power; even so it was suspended by the Vichy government.

The system of government thus had all the elements of instability and tension inherent in a moderately benevolent system of imperial rule. It could not have worked as it did had it not been grafted on to traditional authority. Local administrators – the caids – who exercised administrative, judicial and tax-gathering powers were protected from upheaval, disorder and expropriation in a way they had not been before the French came; but their position was not one to which young ambitious Tunisians would want to succeed. Nationalist aspirations would bring them into conflict with the old order of their own society as well as imperial rule. The apparatus of the State was essentially French and protected settler interests; but the more truly French, and therefore reforming and democratic it became, the more it would meet resistance from its own settlers – without being able to meet the full demands of the nationalists by the surrender of real power.

These sources of tension were only increased by the development of education. Immediately after the occupation it was suggested – by no less than Jules Ferry, the creator of lay education under the third republic – that schooling for the Europeans could be left in the hands of Lavigerie and his missions, and that a greater effort should be made to teach the Tunisians French, and practical trades.

In the event the protectorate created a school system like that in France, primarily for the benefit of the settlers but extended to take in a certain number of the Tunisian population. Primary schools included some which followed exactly the pattern of similar schools in France, staffed by French teachers trained in training colleges in Tunisia; and in addition Franco-Arab schools which taught French, used it as a language of instruction, and also taught Arabic. Secondary education was provided in schools like those in France. But at Sadiki College a special course was provided with an important part given to Arabic studies. Towards the end of the protectorate a variety of this combination was also provided in the most important girls' school, at the leading secondary school – the Lycée Carnot – and at some other schools. There it became possible to work for the 'Sadiki diploma'.

The Catholic religious orders provided schooling for a limited number; the *Alliance israélite* established schools for Jews. Traditional Muslim education remained and was extended. The Zitouna mosque continued to provide its form of higher classical education, and 'annexes' of the Zitouna were established in other towns where the first-year studies could be undertaken. The *kouttabs*, or mosque schools, continued to provide instruction in the Koran, for the most part learning by rote; in addition modern Koranic schools were founded, providing instruction similar to that in the Franco-Arab schools, leading to a certificate, but giving more importance to classical Arabic. These schools were started privately, and later received a subsidy from the state.

The standard of traditional Muslim education, even when the reforms which a young (for the most part French-educated) generation introduced in the twentieth century are taken into account, remained low. At whatever level, it fitted its students only for traditional posts of a relatively unrewarding sort. French schooling was indispensable for advancement under the protectorate – although it was available, as late as 1948, to less than 10 per cent of Tunisians

of school age.[2] The Zitouna school continued to draw its numbers –
but the quality of its students declined and it could offer them neither
decent living conditions, modern education nor a useful qualifica-
tion when they left.

The education most worth aspiring to for young Tunisians was
therefore Sadiki College (or, in the last years of the protectorate, the
Tunisian section of the Lycée Carnot) followed by higher studies in
France. The political effect of this was immense. It created an élite
with a strongly developed national sense, aware of French values. It
brought them into contact with the efficiency of French institutions –
a degree of efficiency which they found attractive but was hardly
likely to overawe them; it also introduced them to a France which
was only weakly represented in the protectorate – the France of
progressive ideas, a socialist party and intellectual freedom. At the
same time it maintained the cohesion of a small group – those who
graduated from Sadiki, those who were in France together, who
were there together during a particular year or who lived through a
sequence of events together. This was in sharp contrast to the
dispersion of an élite which some developing countries have since
allowed (and indeed had thrust upon them) as their students have
gone to Indiana, Uppsala and Cairo.

It was not that the movement for change would not have been
created without the French protectorate – the initial impetus was
given by men who can be seen as the direct successors to Khair-al-
Din. But the current of Islamic reform, in Tunisia, remained weak.
Khair al-Din had been a precursor amongst those Muslim thinkers
who were inspired by the Islamic ideal of a virtuous society and
sought to learn lessons from Europe to re-establish the vigour of
Islam. In the same stream of thought were men like Shaikh Muhammad Abduh, who visited Tunis from Cairo on two occasions, in
1884 and 1903. But the religious élite of Tunisia produced no
comparable thinker, and the one great political leader who emerged
from this class, Shaikh Abdel Aziz Taalbi, was rejected by them
for his radicalism. Moreover the decline of the great religious centres
of the middle ages had taken place long before the Husainid Beys.
Unlike Cairo, Kairouan was isolated from the cross-currents of

trade and civilization which keep thought alive, and this was true to a lesser extent of Tunis itself.

For whatever reason, it was graduates of Sadiki, not of Zitouna, who formed the core of the modernizing and nationalist movement. Taalbi was the exception. It was a Sadiki graduate who in 1888 founded the first Tunisian non-official Arabic language newspaper, *al Hadira*. A group centred on the newspaper also founded an institute in 1896 called the Khalduniya (after the medieval historian and philosopher) designed to provide modern studies for Zitouna students. These were initiatives of major importance. In their immediate context they were in no way revolutionary. Those Tunisians who were interested in modernization in these early years of the protectorate accepted French rule as unchangeable, and confined their demands on the government to such things as the employment of more Tunisians in minor positions in the government. The Khalduniya was started with the active support of the Resident-General, and against the opposition of the ulema. But a major step in self-help and organization had been taken, in education, with all its implications both for the development of ideas and for ever-increasing demands which in the long run could only be met by the state.

Out of the Khalduniya grew the important movement of the turn of the century known as the Young Tunisians, with its own newspaper, *Le Tunisien*, founded in 1907 (an Arabic version followed under the direction of Taalbi in 1909). The Young Tunisians were few in number. They came from an aristocracy which found itself denied access to government as a result of the protectorate. Many of them came from the Mameluke class – not those whose families still enjoyed status and local power in rural Tunisia, but the sons of those who had formed a governing class under the Beys. Of the two foremost contributors to *Le Tunisien* one, Ali Bach Hamba, was Turkish, the other, Abdel Jelil Zaouche, had received a French education and wrote classical Arabic with difficulty.

Even so the movement was not nationalist (few aristocratic movements are). It accepted the French protectorate, and sought the extension of the benefits of the protectorate to Tunisians in every way. They wanted more French education, not to the exclusion of Arabic but as the means to modernization and to give Tunisians greater access to government employment (Ali Bach Hamba argued that Arabic was an inadequate medium for modernization). In 1910 an article in *Le Tunisien* suggested naturalization (with the maintenance of Muslim jurisdiction over matters of personal status such as marriage) as the best solution for the problems of North Africa.[3] They pressed strongly for what they called indigenous colonization – that is to say for Tunisians to be able to benefit from the land laws and from the facilities provided by the government to help the introduction of modern methods of agriculture.

Before the foundation of *Le Tunisien* two members of the movement had gone to a colonial conference held by the French in Marseilles in 1906. This had given them an excellent opportunity to develop their programme. In addition it had brought them more directly in contact with French opinion. They were encouraged to find the extent of support which their ideas received from radical sections of French politics – as well they might, for their programme was well reasoned, coherent and flattering to the French. It fitted the assimilationist idea which was at the centre of French imperial thought. Henceforth there would be three ranks of Frenchmen facing the Tunisian reformers and nationalists – the settlers, who would be the most resistant to them, the protectorate government which at least had a responsibility for the country as a whole, and beyond the protectorate, public opinion in France.

Meanwhile the Young Tunisians had embraced an idea of the state which was remote from and ignored Islamic theory and traditional Tunisian practice. As Carl Brown has shown, their prime concern was with efficiency rather than democracy, and they believed that the state must take responsibility for organizing society. Their dominant concern was with education, and in spite of their own contribution in the Khalduniya, they realized that the extension of education could only come from the state. Many of them were hesitant about the value of the reformed Koranic schools, which they believed could not make sufficient progress in modern education. In this and every respect of their political thinking they were in a different world from the limited state machine and the social role of the mosque and religious brotherhoods.

In the early years of the twentieth century there thus existed a cohesive body of modernizers, closely linked amongst themselves, having the organization of the newspaper, the Khalduniya and an association of *anciens élèves* from Sadiki. But their organization came to an abrupt end just before the first world war, and when that war was over conditions and the current of opinion in Tunisia had changed fundamentally. The immediate cause of the demise of the movement was trivial. The Young Tunisians sponsored a boycott of the street-cars in Tunis in March 1912 in pursuit of equal pay for Tunisian workers and better treatment of Tunisian passengers. In response the government arrested seven of the leaders and deported four – Ali Bach Hamba died in Constantinople in 1918. The war and martial law came before the movement could reorganize itself.

There is no more powerful catalyst to social change and the growth of a reforming ideology than war. The first world war was not fought on Tunisian soil, as the second was; but it took some 100,000 Tunisians away to fight or work and inflicted casualties on 40,000 of them. This meant that from all over the country men were taken out from their traditional environment, where they would be likely to accept what they found (including the established system of political authority) and returned as a fertile field for new demands; and it meant that the politically alert members of the nation would respond to the ideals of self-determination which were propagated by President Wilson. A group of Tunisians reacted sufficiently to the European political atmosphere to try to send a delegation to the Paris peace conference.

The settler community and the protectorate government were going in the opposite direction. The pioneering character of the early years had now given way to an increasingly defensive position. The returns from agriculture had ceased to increase or were declining; wine growers found themselves in competition with their countrymen in the south of France, the acreage was limited and some vines pulled up. Farming called increasingly on the assistance of the state in finance and in technical knowledge to fill inadequacies which had revealed themselves in happy-go-lucky farming. The settler bourgeoisie was on the defensive against its own socialists and workers – who in turn wanted to retain their primacy over the Tunisians. The country which used the legal fiction of a protectorate to occupy Tunisia, which had instituted legal tribunals as a powerful force of modernization, was now a conservative colonial power, defending established institutions against the legalistic attacks of the Tunisians. The age of Lavigerie had given way to that of his statue.

In these circumstances the nationalist movement took a striking turn. A new party was established, called the Destour, and a book published in Paris called *La Tunisie Martyre*. The leader of the party and the presumed author of the book was Shaikh Abdel Aziz Taalbi. He made a link with the Young Tunisians – he had attended courses at the Khalduniya and edited the Arabic *Tunisien*. But while the Young Tunisians had admired French government and efficiency, Taalbi attacked the French with bitterness and looked back to a golden age before the protectorate – the age of the Constitution of 1861, from which the name of the party was given.

The Destour movement has been described as backward-looking; more perceptively Jacques Berque has said: 'Le pamphlet de *La Tunisie Martyre* vaut moins par l'analyse que par la préscience.'[4] Addressed to a French audience, it claims that the Tunisian state before the protectorate embodied the values to which French political theory attached most importance – separation of powers, social contract, declaration of the rights and duties of man. In contrast the regime of the protectorate had none of these qualities. It was as alien to the Tunisian nation as Chinese civilization to French; it was a grievous and heavy burden for Tunisia to bear, morally, politically and economically. One of many passages of bitter nationalism is that which complains that, when the Tunisians wanted instruction in science, they were given instead the French primary school. It continues:

For one people to try to make another people – one lacking organization and being of different faith and race – accept an ideal is an exceptionally difficult undertaking; but when the society it attacks is organized (as is the case with our Tunisia), has an historic past and its own civilization; when it is, moreover, a society which reveres its own history and civilization whose rich‑ness and virtues have been well‑tried; when the aggressors use brutality and oppression; then the enterprise is doomed to failure: the fury of the oppressors is aroused and translated into moral violence which, without enhancing the prestige of the aggressors, disturbs people's minds and increases, with all the horror of its sterility, the sum of crimes against humanity.

This strident yet syncretic nationalism – for it unconsciously em‑bodied the ideals of the society it attacked – was an indispensable ingredient of the national self‑awareness which must precede independence.

Yet the nationalist movement as a whole was full of confusion and false starts. The Destour party itself had no clear plan of action. It lacked the nerve and the resources to be an out‑and‑out revo‑lutionary party vowed to the overthrow of the protectorate, and it lacked the political acumen to make political capital out of other‑wise trivial incidents. It drew up a long list of 'demands' and then rested its case. Although its branch organization spread in the 1920's it was ineffective in building widespread popular feeling into a mass party. The leaders of the Destour came primarily from Tunis and were drawn from the traditional governing class of religious lawyers and well‑to‑do merchants. The new atmosphere of the twenties, with the protests of the élite being taken up by ordinary people, but such people only partially organized by the Destour, has been described by Berque:

Let us picture a meeting of the Destour party at Mahdia in 1922. Scarcely, as yet, a 'cell', but a gathering of some twenty or thirty people, grocers, hairdressers, chauffeurs, mechanics from the har‑bour, a few students from the Zaituna, even a petty leader. A few years later, at Tunis in 1929, a blind baker held a meeting in his bakehouse: the cause of the excitement was the detention of Guefrash, one of the 1925 protesters, who was in prison for having demonstrated at Gabès in favour of Abd el‑Krim. There was talk of imprisonments and protests and petitions. Wild hopes were raised.[4]

Other incidents and persons of the 1920's showed future potential as yet unrealized. The French trade-union organization, the CGT – still at this time a socialist, not communist organization – assumed that Tunisian workers would join the French unions, without trying very hard to persuade them to do so. Suddenly in 1924 an independent Tunisian union emerged, to be suppressed by the protectorate. It was created by a man named Mohamed Ali, who spent one year of his adult life in Tunisia at this time. While abroad he had formed romantic ideas about the possibility of Tunisian development; coming back to Tunisia he had tried to establish cooperatives; then moved to the organization of discontented dock-workers in Tunis. Rapidly a Confédération générale des travailleurs tunisiens was formed and secured the adherence of dockers, street-car workers, municipal employees and others; it spread from Tunis to Sfax, Bizerte and other towns, organizing strikes and demonstra-tions – until it was suppressed and Mohamed Ali exiled. (He later became a driver between Jedda and Mecca, and died at the wheel.) The weakness of the Destour was amply demonstrated by its aloof-ness from this flowering of national working-class organization. In contrast a small communist party had tried to take advantage of the breakaway movement and had assisted its organization. As for the labour movement itself, it was given no chance to reappear until 1937; when it did it was a powerful contributor to the movement for independence.

Meanwhile Mohamed Ali had his biographer in the person of a radical reformer named Tahar Haddad, who analysed Tunisian society in strongly Marxist terms. He also published a book on the position of women in Islamic society, pressing for the emancipation of women to the extent of causing a scandal, which lost him his job at the Zitouna university and evoked the publication of a number of books in reply to his thesis. Relatively unimportant politically, Haddad's career shows the conflict between modernism and nationalism. Thirty years later the Néo-Destourian government of Tunisia gave prime importance to the position of women in society; but at this time they were unable to come wholeheartedly to Haddad's support. Modernism of his variety, attacking a deeply ingrained Muslim institution, could do little to serve the cause of national independence.

It was at this time, in the middle of these confused and conflicting initiatives in modernization and nationalism, that a new party emerged under the leadership of Habib Bourguiba. Its novelty did not lie in a reconciliation of the ideological differences between different strands of Tunisian thought; it was rather in organization and tactics. It was assisted in this by the economic situation, which continued to deteriorate and was made very much worse when the world slump struck France and its colonies in 1932 – at a time too of bad harvests, which have always been powerful catalysts in political history.

The traditional leadership of the Destour ran into the sand during the 1920's. Having done so much to create nationalist feeling and to express a nationalist case they were unable or unwilling to proceed further. Younger men – Mahmoud Materi, Tahar Sfar and Habib Bourguiba – pressed impatiently for a more vigorous and demanding attitude and for action against the protectorate. They ran a new newspaper, *La Voix du Tunisien*, in which they angrily attacked the French president, Doumergue, during his visit of 1931; two years later they founded a new paper, significantly called *L'Action Tunisienne*. In March 1934 the final break came, and at a historic conference held at Ksar Hellal the Néo-Destour party was formed.

Ksar Hellal is a small town in the Sahel – the coastal area between Sousse and Mahdia – about twelve miles from Bourguiba's birthplace in Monastir. The revolt of the Néo-Destour came from a new social group. The old Destour had been led by men coming from the old families of Tunis: they had always been close to the governments of the Bey and of the French, and the city in which they lived had the traditional core of urban Islam – the Zitouna mosque and the souks of the medina. At its side were first the funduks of foreign merchants, then the French government and a modern French town built around the medina. The leaders of the Néo-Destour, in contrast, came from a part of the country which had not been colonized, which had a profound North African character of its own. It was a village society where Islam had mingled with older traditions and where orthodoxy was tempered by popular mysticism, where the ethos of society was compounded of family and ancestral ties, a not very pious or devout acceptance of religion, and social customs stronger in force than religion itself. Coming from this background, the Néo-Destour also knew France; but the France they knew had been revealed to them at Sadiki and then experienced at first hand in Paris, in the atmosphere of commitment and rigour characteristic of the intellectual left.

Themselves belonging to this new class, they were ready to seek support from others who had not previously entered into politics, from whom the Destour had remained remote. The effect of the French occupation had been to create a proletariat, urban and rural – peasants driven from the land by the development of French and large Tunisian estates, urban poor drawn into the towns by the prospect of a slightly higher standard of living, men working in the docks or the mines. (The Tunisian dockers, who had already formed the core of the CGTT, invited political organization – industrial workers, they were drawn from a single oasis near Gabès and combined group loyalty with working-class resentment.) Even the southern tribes suffered as a result of colonization – historically they had survived bad periods by incursions into the settled area of the coast, and this was denied to them by the establishment of French law and order. The material for modern political organiza-tion was thus readily available; inspired by such examples as the French socialist party the Néo-Destour took advantage of it.

Organization was accompanied by tactics – tactics which may be described as unremitting gradualist pressure. The stone wellheads in the courtyard of the Kairouan mosque are deeply worn by the fibres of rope, pulled up and down often enough – and this was the simile which Bourguiba used to describe his political action. The Néo-Destour was advancing on two fronts: it sought independence, and it wanted far-reaching reforms of Tunisian society. On both fronts it proceeded step by step.

In doing so it accepted compromises, especially in the last years when independence was in sight. But Bourguiba and his colleagues showed political sense in accepting compromise which provided them with the levers for further advance, but never compromise which emasculated their own movement. They recognized that they had not the strength for a bloody frontal attack but equally that the gradualist approach must be advanced enough to represent a challenge to French authority, that the French would inevitably respond with repressive measures which would include their imprisonment and exile, and that their personal commitment as well as their organizational strength must be adequate to overcome such repression. In fact their success in this regard was crowned by the growth of a political emotion – of widespread commitment on the part of ordinary people in Néo-Destour cells to the cause of independence, led by Bourguiba as the 'Supreme Combatant' or (in Arabic) 'the greatest of the fighters in the holy war'.

The immediate issue which had preceded the break of the Néo-Destour from the old party had been the question of the right of naturalized Tunisians (under a law of 1923) to burial in Muslim cemeteries. Over a large perspective the Néo-Destour has been a secularizing party, and as soon as it achieved independence passed a law on personal status which established civil codes and ended religious custom in a way the French had not dared to do. But in 1933 it was the young militants of the Destour party who took the view that those who accepted French citizenship thereby excluded themselves from the Muslim community and forfeited the right to burial in Muslim cemeteries; they supported the Mufti of Bizerte who took this stand and opposed the rector of Zitouna, who (to serve the French) issued a *fetwa* in the opposite sense. Similarly Bourguiba at this stage supported the use of the veil as another distinctive sign of Tunisian nationality – it was after independence that he called it 'a filthy rag'.

These were attitudes appropriate to a party which looked for mass support. The Néo-Destour leaders distinguished themselves by the way in which they avoided the isolation of so many of the intelligentsia from their own people. *Anciens élèves* of Sadiki worked together with Zitouna graduates, and both retained contact with people who, without necessarily being very devout, accepted the practices of Islam as a part of a deeply ingrained pattern of life. In many other countries – starting from Russia in the nineteenth century – the intelligentsia discovered their ideals in another country and another civilization, in another language, and were thereby cut off from the peasants and the workpeople in their own country. This danger the Néo-Destour avoided.

The party needed all the strength it could muster. Of the twenty years which followed the formation of the Néo-Destour in March 1934 until the promise of autonomy in 1954, Bourguiba spent half in prison. The party itself was dissolved six months after its formation; thereafter it was tolerated during the period of the Popular Front of 1936, and at the end of the war. Even then it did not have legal existence and toleration could be ended abruptly – as it was in January 1952.

Only during the government of Léon Blum in 1936, when Pierre Viénot was Under-Secretary of State, did a significant liberalization of French imperial policy seem possible – not only in North Africa but in the Middle East. Following an established pattern of imperial rule the French government allowed Taalbi to return to Tunisia after he had ceased to represent the mainstream of nationalist opposition – there were now some four hundred Néo-Destour cells throughout the country and Taalbi was met with derision and insult.

The liberalization of empire which the Popular Front proposed, limited as it was, aroused the fierce opposition of the French Chamber, and the government itself broke up in 1937. There followed a period of conflict in Tunisia. Rioting in Bizerte opened a series of clashes which culminated in a demonstration in Tunis on 9 April 1938, when government troops fired on the crowd and killed some 122 persons. The day passed into national history as Martyrs' Day.

The Tunisian trade-union organization was dissolved, the Néo-Destour outlawed and Bourguiba imprisoned. But in spite of repression he realized that self-government could only be given to Tunisia by the French; and he never despaired of the idea that the people he knew in France were sympathetic to him. He therefore always made an appeal to the French and spoke of the need for cooperation between Tunisia and France – at no time was this more striking than during the second world war. With the fall of France, Bourguiba was taken from his confinement in Tunisia to prison at Marseilles, where he remained until the allied landings in North Africa, when he was taken by the Germans to Rome. Before this latter move – and, more significantly, before the victories of Alamein and Stalingrad, which marked the turning point of the war – Bourguiba wrote a letter (published by the Tunisians after the war) to Dr Habib Thamer, on 8 August 1942:

> Give the militants the order – on my responsibility and *even over my signature* if necessary – to enter into relations with Gaullist France in Tunisia (there must certainly be some: certain of our socialist friends, for example) with a view to joining if possible our clandestine action with theirs and leaving aside for after the war the problem of our independence.
>
> Try if possible, and through their connection, to enter into contact with the British or American agents who must abound in Tunisia. They can be sounded on the intentions of their countries towards us after the victory.[6]

Similarly in May 1943 he wrote 'Faîtes bloc aujourd'hui avec la France, il n'est pas de salut hors la France.'[7]

Bourguiba's coldness to Italian seduction and his refusal to co-operate with the Axis contrasted sharply with the flaccid behaviour of the French Resident-General.[8] In November 1942, a month after El Alamein, American and British forces landed in Morocco and Algeria in operation 'Torch'. Their plan was to push eastwards and clear the north coast of Africa of the Axis armies. But rain delayed their advance and they were unable to capture Bizerte or Tunis.

For the time being they had failed to pass the strategic line of the Mediterranean, which had been of such vital importance between Spaniards and Turks some four centuries earlier. Across the straits from Sicily nearly 30,000 German troops and their equipment were transported by sea and air. As a result some of the bitterest battles of the North African campaign were fought in Tunisia. The Free French forces of General Leclerc, as well as New Zealand and Indian troops, fought with the British and Americans.

In February the Germans counterattacked, unsuccessfully, at Sidi Bou Zid and the Kasserine pass. Then, as the weather improved, the Allied forces were able to advance, defeating the German and Italian armies at Mareth and Médenine, then at Wadi Akarit. The remaining Axis forces were now surrounded, and it was a matter of time before their bridgehead at Tunis fell to the Allies. On 13 May 1943 General Alexander reported to Churchill, 'We are masters of the North African shores'. The way was open for a fresh invasion, following the path of the Hafsids, from Tunis to Sicily. Bourguiba's confidence in allied victory, only matched by his antipathy to the Axis, proved justified.

The political rewards for his sagacity were indirect and delayed. While Bourguiba had been in exile the succession of the Beylicate had passed to Moncef Bey. In the crucial years of 1942–3 he had played his cards as well as a ruling monarch could hope to do in the circumstances – pressing for concessions from Vichy, then, as Vichy authority disintegrated, forming a national government. With the return of the French he was forced to abdicate and never returned to the throne. The strength of the Beylicate was thus weakened, for Moncef died in 1948 and his successor could not take up the aura which had surrounded a national martyr. Taalbi too died in 1944, and Bourguiba was left as the unrivalled leader of Tunisian nationalism.

At the same time the nationalist movement had acquired increased strength through the emergence of an autonomous labour movement. In January 1946 the Union Générale Tunisienne du Travail (UGTT) was formed, open to workers of any nationality but in practice a Tunisian movement, under the leadership of Ferhat Hached. It had two reasons for establishing its independence from the CGT – the first that the French union wanted to preserve the dominance of French workers, the second that it had come under communist domination after the war. The UGTT pursued an independent course. It affiliated briefly with the World Federation of Trade Unions, but when the world labour movement split with the development of the cold war it joined the anti-communist International Confederation of Free Trade Unions. In so doing it had the strong support of the American labour movement, and it gave the Tunisians access to an American and an international forum to argue the case for independence. Bourguiba and Ferhat Hached attended the AFL conference at San Francisco in 1951, and when Bahi Ladgham went to New York on behalf of the Néo-Destour to establish a Tunisian Office for National Liberation he was assisted by the AFL.[9] The French government was forced into arbitrary decisions affecting the participation of the Tunisians in the international labour movement – not allowing Ferhat Hached to go to New York in 1952, but allowing a delegation to go to the ICFTU congress in Stockholm the next year. Between these two events a terrorist organization of the French settlers acted brutally against the UGTT by assassinating Ferhat Hached, in December 1952.

Meanwhile successive French governments yielded little to the demands of Tunisian nationalism. Returning to power after the war, de Gaulle interpreted the greatness of France as that of an imperial power; a decade or more was to pass before he accepted decolonization as a means to greatness in Europe and the world. After his resignation in January 1946 the governments of the Fourth Republic attempted a mixture of repression and moderate reforms in the Middle East, Madagascar and North Africa. The crucial years were those of 1950–52. The Tunisian government under the premiership of Sidi Mohamed Chenik – which included Salah ben Youssef as Minister of Justice – pressed the French government for reform which would provide internal autonomy. Instead the French replied in February 1951 with proposals for co-sovereignty, which alarmed the settlers and conservative interests in France without pleasing the Tunisians. A French election in June 1951 brought a more conservative Assembly, and fresh proposals which were put forward at the end of the year made little concession to the Tunisian demands. In France itself the proposals were vigorously criticized by the socialists – and by Michel Debré.[10]

Meanwhile Bourguiba had been abroad, seeking international support for the Tunisian cause. At the end of the second world war he had left Tunisia secretly and gone to Cairo, returning in 1949. In the spring of 1950 he went to Paris, and the following year to India, Pakistan, Indonesia, the United States – while Salah ben Youssef represented the Néo-Destour in the Tunisian government. In December 1951 he denounced the French government's proposals and regarded the attempt to negotiate as finished for the time being. In January 1952 he was arrested by the new Resident-General, de Hautecloque, and sent to Tabarka, later to the south of the country. The French carried out a vigorous police action. The Resident-General used his semi-independent powers to the full; the moderate Tunisian prime minister and his colleagues were dismissed and placed under house arrest; arrests and deportations were followed by strikes and demonstrations, which were met by further repression. The murder of Ferhat Hached came at the end of a year of violence.

The change in French policy came in 1954. Until that time France had appeared committed to the defence of a modernized imperial position throughout the world – one which would give varying degrees of self-government or, as in the Tunisian case, extended participation of the indigenous population, while retaining a federative principle for the Union as a whole. But governments of the fourth republic were weak, formed as a result of compromise in a multi-party system. They were particularly weak in their administration of overseas territories. They were vulnerable to pressures from French settlers; the control they exercised over their own representatives, civilian and military, was incomplete. Hautecloque's arrest of Chenik and his ministers was not, as far as is known, ordered from Paris; in Morocco the Sultan was deposed in a similar manner in 1953 (although the strength of nationalist opinion forced his reinstatement two years later).

In South-East Asia, France had gone much further than in North Africa in the extension of self-government. Laos and Cambodia were autonomous states, and a nationalist government had been set up under Bao Dai in Vietnam. Even so the French had been at war with the Vietminh and were fighting a losing battle in an attempt to establish Bao Dai's rule over the country as a whole. In the summer of 1954 the deepening crisis led to the collapse of one of the longest-lived but most indecisive of the governments of the Fourth Republic, that of Joseph Laniel. He was succeeded by Pierre Mendès-France, who, at the Geneva conference, negotiated a settlement of Indo-China. He also went to Tunisia, visited the Bey and on 31 July 1954 proclaimed the self-government of Tunisia. From his French prison Bourguiba described the Mendès-France proposal as a 'substantial and decisive stage on the way to the restoration of the complete sovereignty of Tunisia'. Independence, he said, remained the ideal of the Tunisian people; but the movement towards independence would now be made 'by close cooperation between the two peoples, conscious of their solidarity – cooperation from which all ideas of domination will be banished.'[11]

It took nearly a year to negotiate the terms of Tunisia's internal sovereignty. They were embodied in Conventions signed in June 1955, protecting French interests, especially in education. In the event they were the prelude to a rapid acceleration of the grant of complete independence. In French policy a distinction was now made between the two North African protectorates of Tunisia and Morocco, and Algeria. In Morocco the failure of the attempt to depose Mohamed V and suppress the nationalist movement was followed by the negotiation of independence, and this was quickly followed by complete independence for Tunisia in March 1956.

The manner in which independence had been achieved was of vital importance to the future of the country. It had been won with some struggle. There were notable martyrs to the cause of independence, like Ferhat Hached; and there were many unknown martyrs, ordinary people who had been killed in struggles with the army and police, many others who had suffered deportation or imprisonment. Yet society had never collapsed into anarchy or taken on the character of civil war. There had been no openings for the violent extremism which flourishes in such a situation.

At the same time the forces of moderate nationalism had also weakened. Tunisians of the old order had in varying degrees fought their own battle with the French, from a very different position.

Men like Moncef Bey, Mohamed Chenik, his successor Tahar ben Ammar had pressed for the extension of self-government in the confined role which the French allowed them. With such men the French could have negotiated internal autonomy at any time from the popular front onwards, and the history of Tunisia would have been very different as a result. In 1956 they were a spent political force.

Bourguiba had been in prison during the early part of the nego/tiations for the Conventions, and was then brought to Paris, still under supervision, but in practice part of the Tunisian delegation. When he returned to Tunis in 1955 he was given a hero's welcome. He faced a single challenge which was offered by Salah ben Youssef and overcame it. He was then the undisputed leader of a vigorous and modern political organization; and the man who could justly claim that his strategy and dedication over a score of years had won independence in cooperation with France.

8 Bourguiba

HABIB BOURGUIBA IS UNIQUE amongst modern political leaders. Before the war of 1939 he was the outstanding director and animator of his country's movement for independence. He has sur‑ vived the natural hazards of mortal life and has emerged dominant from the vicissitudes of political strife. He has earned the honour and respect of his own people. He is called and calls himself the father of the nation and the supreme combatant. In almost every other new country of the world the pre‑war nationalists have disappeared, whether peacefully like Nehru or in violence like Nuri as‑Said. Only King Idris of Libya rivalled the continuity of anti‑imperial struggle and independent leadership of Bourguiba.

Bourguiba's youth and his early career were similar to those of many who worked with him in the Néo‑Destour movement. They are entirely appropriate to the formation of a nationalist leader, to the growth of nationalist feeling and the development of a will to political action. But they offer little clue to the exceptional role which Bourguiba was to play.

He was born on 3 August 1903, at Monastir – in the heart of the Sahel. His grandfather and uncle took part in the rebellion of 1864; his father was a lieutenant in the Bey's army. His mother died while he was an infant, and at the age of five he was sent to Tunis, where his brother Mohamed took responsibility for him. He entered the primary school annex of Sadiki College and then, in 1913, entered the College itself as a boarder.

His education was interrupted by a spell of tuberculosis, then resumed at the French secondary school, the Lycée Carnot. While still at school he joined the Destour and was in trouble because of his political activity; but he passed the baccalaureate examination nonetheless. Sadiki College gave him a small grant to continue his studies in Paris, where he inscribed at the Law Faculty and the School of Political Science.

His education in Tunis and Paris did much to form his personality and outlook. It took him out of his local surroundings, and placed his background in the larger perspective of the history and thought of Europe as well as Islam. He grew up as a humanist, rejecting Marxism, sensitive to the ideals of a socialism designed to provide individuals with wider scope for self-development, attracted to Comte and Renan. He made friends not only amongst other North Africans but amongst Frenchmen. He went through the experience of innumerable young people from colonial territories in discovering that France was not inhabited by colonial civil servants. He came to be aware of a liberal and radical French tradition.

He returned to Tunis in 1927 and entered the bar; in a very short time he also began writing, as the obvious entry to a political career. He predicted the end of the protectorate, for, he said, a state cannot remain subject and sovereign. Either it will grow steadily more defunct until it is absorbed by the protecting power; or alternatively, if the nation brought under protectorate is

> a healthy vigorous people, whom international rivalries or a momentary crisis have forced to accept the tutelage of a strong state, then the necessarily inferior situation which it is placed in, the contact with a more advanced civilization brings about a salutary reaction: under the spur of necessity which is bound up with the instinct of survival . . . a veritable regeneration is produced; and, thanks to a judicious assimilation of the principles and methods of this civilization it will inevitably succeed in realizing by stages its final emancipation.[1]

Mortality must one day deprive Tunisia of Bourguiba. Meanwhile the system, the style and the ethos of Tunisian politics are centred on him. In the past he has taken key decisions which have determined the strategy and tactics of the nationalist movement; he continues

to make decisions of government. He is responsible for appoint/
ments, and makes them from a knowledge of all the leading
personalities of his country. The older generation are known to him
intimately from the struggle they shared; he has taken trouble to
know the younger men who now hold governorships or other key
positions. His past and his position make available to him, in a
small country, personal knowledge of his lieutenants which none of
them can rival. He has long believed in the value of direct contact
with the people and so expends his energies in speaking to large and
small meetings, on radio and on television. In these speeches and in
the practice of government which he has animated he has established
a rough/hewn political ethos.

It is an ethos which stops short of an ideology. It lays no claim to
be based on a scientific interpretation of history and society. Although
it is constructed on certain widely accepted moral tenets it is not
offered as being universally applicable to societies other than Tunisia.

Pragmatism plays a key part in this ethos. Again and again
Bourguiba has insisted on the 'need not for ideology but for practical
achievement'. He has condemned ideology as a lure and a scapegoat.
Men 'must assume responsibility for their acts' and not load 'respon/
sibility for our failures on the back of such scapegoats as neo/
colonialism, imperialism and reaction'. The theme is repeated with
variations appropriate to the audience and the occasion. The
ideological commission of the Destourian Party is told that 'it is not
by living in the Latin quarter or by plunging into ideologies that
one comes to understand the realities of a country.' Speaking to the
University of Tunis, Bourguiba has drawn a contrast between the
universalist nature of knowledge, and the practical aspects of learning
and action. 'Man finds his accomplishment only insofar as he
reflects on his temporal and spatial roots, integrates himself in the
reality surrounding him, derives nourishment from it and inter/
mingles with it, to the point where his being coincides with its
reality and this reality is transformed into a flow of creative energy
from his being.'

The continuity between the struggle for independence and the
problems of the new state is interpreted in a way that is consistent

with this pragmatism. The catchwords and jargons of demagogy have no place in Bourguiba's speech. Instead he talks repeatedly of the continuing struggle to achieve true independence The struggle for independence from France began (for Bourguiba) thirty-five years ago, political independence came ten years ago; but the struggle to escape from the dictates of harsh nature, the inadequacies of natural resources, the shortcomings of a still uneducated and untrained people – this struggle continues. Bourguiba's exhortations fit well into the picture which Michelet drew of human history more than a century ago, when he described the course of human events as a perpetual battle of liberty against fatality.

An ethos necessarily involves certain assumptions about human nature. Bourguiba's assumptions are that men are susceptible to reasonable arguments, that they are improvable if not perfectible. Only with reluctance and very rarely has he accepted that political quarrels need endure; those whom he has overcome in a struggle for power he expects to be reintegrated into useful work at a later date. 'To convince rather than to coerce and to prevent rather than to cure', as part of 'a national movement based not on the cult of violence but, on the contrary, on the idea that we should work for the triumph of reason and right, with dignity and respect for human values.' 'Is not reason the greatest power God has given to man?' asked Bourguiba in a speech in Beirut in March 1965 – reason (as he went on to explain) not in its natural state, bestowed equally on all men, but reason developed and fostered, forged into an instru-ment to 'subjugate the forces of nature and dominate the course of events'.

The importance of this ethos cannot be overestimated. Ethos or ideology provides the lubricant for developing societies, making possible the harnessing of energy with the minimum of friction. Ideology may be dogmatic, and subject to interpretation only by a supposedly infallible leadership; it will normally create distant horizons towards which the people are urged – horizons which inevitably recede as swiftly as the people advance. With such an ideology the Soviet Union was industrialized. The ethos which Bourguiba has given Tunisia is different. Reason and argument are an essential part of it – even though central direction remains decisive. Movement forward is not towards the distant and elusive horizon of a millennium; instead it is progress stage by stage – *étape par étape*. Independence itself was one stage of development, and a major one at that; but there were others before and have been others since. To achieve independence one studied politics, law and history, formed a party, struggled for power, and made compro/mises until strong enough to take complete control. To bring barren land into use one carries out research, plants small trees which grow into big trees, plants crops in their shelter. Stage by stage the process is the same.

The objective of such development is not a utopian form of society nor is it merely increased material wealth; it is human dignity and moral betterment. In Bourguiba's exhortations anything and everything may contribute to this end – dress, education, freedom of thought, work. Men cannot have self/respect unless they are dressed and shaved in a seemly manner; human dignity is im/possible in conditions of poverty and penury; moral betterment consists in freeing men – and even more, women – from old taboos and replacing them with discipline which is self/imposed. 'Real independence means independence at the service of the people for its betterment.' Each person's dignity is increased as he strives for the betterment of others. 'The motto "Live for others", which is written on the base of Auguste Comte's bust in the courtyard of the Sor/bonne, made a strong impression on me when I was a young student in Paris. It has been my motto through life,' Bourguiba told the medical profession in June 1966.

Samuel Smiles would find himself at home in Bourguiba's world. Work is given a high moral value for itself, as well as for what it achieves. On the first of May 1966 it was not the working class or the proletariat or the socialist movement which drew Bourguiba's praise. Instead he claimed: 'To our credit we have rehabilitated work.' In a colonial society work appeared as the stigma attached to second/class citizens; and there was a limit to the rewards it could bring; but 'in our times what ennobles man is work'. The cadres and leadership of the country are presented as working arduously for the growth of their country – and justly so, as anyone familiar with the habits of Tunisian ministers wlll testify. So it is for the people as a whole. 'Money cannot drop down from heaven as a bounty. You will earn your bread by the sweat of your brow.' Here indeed is the lubricant which has made possible an economic policy of holding wages down to restrict consumer demand and promote investment.

Islam is also invoked in support of the sanctity of work. The Arabic newspaper, *Al Amal*, prints the Koranic verse, 'Counsel them to devote themselves to a useful activity; God, as well as the Prophet and all believers, will be pleased with them.' But Islam does not dominate the Tunisian ethos. It is rather a minor theme in a syncretic morality which draws much from nineteenth-century Europe. Too much in Islamic tradition and practice is an impedi-ment to the exercise of human will and the endeavour to change society which are central themes of Bourguibism. As Clifford Geertz has written, 'Muhammad's followers live now not so much in the brilliant glare of religious innovation as in the half-light of doctrinal orthodoxy.'² Too often the mood of Islam has been fatalistic resignation – though that it is not necessarily so is evident from the combination of devoutness and enterprise found at Sfax.

Bourguiba has invoked the Koran and Hadith in praise of work, in condemnation of divorce, in justification of the public ownership of water; and on the occasion of the visit of King Faisal of Saudi Arabia he spoke of Tunisia's Arabo-Islamic vocation. But signifi-cantly in a speech to mark the anniversary of the founding of the Néo-Destour party he quoted the French Commissioner Peyrouton who had said: 'There is nobility in the attitude of the Moslem submissive to his destiny, but there is supreme nobility in that of the Westerner who wants to be the artificer of his destiny.' And Bourguiba continued: 'This fatalistic resignation, which I consider to be contrary to the true spirit of Islam, was changed by us on 3rd January 1934 into a determination to change the world, into faith in our methods of action, into creative enthusiasm.'

There have been several occasions when Bourguiba has sought to change not only the mood of Islam, but practices which have a central place in the religious practice – most important of them the fast of Ramadan. With more or less success he has sought to effect change in the name of 'the true spirit of Islam'. He has justly said (at a banquet given by King Faisal of Saudi Arabia): 'Islam is a whole from which neither the temporal nor the spiritual may be dissociated': but he uses his political authority as far as he can to bend religious practice.

Bourguiba rarely makes direct reference to the Tunisian nation. He makes no spurious claim to superiority on behalf of the Tunisians. The nation is referred to rather as the society to which all citizens belong; and the duty, responsibility and commitment of the citizens to the nation as a society is a recurrent theme. He is obviously aware and frequently refers to the part which he and the Néo-Destour party played in creating a nation – 'we have forged a disordered mass of individuals into a nation' – but the essence of the nation is that men take responsibility for the affairs of the whole society. 'Every citizen is responsible for the destiny of the nation.'

While the goal of all political and economic activity is moral betterment and human dignity, this can only be achieved through the development of society. Every individual and every organization thus has its 'social function'. Traders and farmers are no different in this respect from lawyers and doctors; 'To all I speak to, I recommend that they work militantly to bring about a homogeneous, harmonious and constantly progressing society.' Similarly the state is given a social function – 'The only purpose of State intervention is to vindicate justice, to improve productivity, to encourage investments.' The sentiment is noble; in practice the state seeks first to maintain its own authority, but even so the nebulous concept of its 'social function' does affect the habits and style of government.

Bourguiba has never hesitated to talk of himself and his own role in the construction of the Tunisian nation and present government of his country. He often talks of himself in the third person – a habit which is the more curious when it occurs in private conversation. He is accused of vanity and the language in which he speaks of himself at first sight provides justification for the charge. Certainly Bourguiba cannot view the development of his country except as centring on himself – but nor can anyone else. He regards himself as the agent who has brought his country to independence and beyond, and as a model whom others could emulate; but he does not think of himself as the incarnation of Tunisia or the quintessence, in some mystical sense, of his nation. He believes himself to be able to inspire, not fear, but only 'love and gratitude' amongst his people.

For Bourguiba as for others the Tunisian nation is still a fragile construction. The Tunisian past is not one of brilliant political success. 'Throughout history', as Bourguiba has said, 'Tunisia has offered the spectacle of a country unceasingly torn apart by revolts, fratricidal struggles and insurrections followed by bloody repression.' History therefore gives no reason for an optimistic assumption that the country will be free of the upheaval, turmoil and strife which have torn apart other Arab and African countries. The conclusion which Bourguiba draws from this is that he should keep power in his own hands; both because this is the only safe way to lay the foundation for democracy; and because as he, Bourguiba, took the right decisions in the movement towards independence he can best be relied on to take the right decisions in the future. 'Some may obviously wonder whether it be prudent to let the destiny of a country depend on the flashes of genius of one man. But what else can be done? A great nation like France has now a long democratic tradition; but it has arrived at this point, after centuries, because of the service which monarchy rendered to the country in maintaining its unity despite its internal struggles.'

While retaining control in his own hands Bourguiba does not overlook what must be done to ensure the perpetuation of a stable society based on reason and consent. He has said: 'The sole ambition of Bourguiba, who is only 'passing through' on this earth, is to train men.' Again and again he returns to the need to train cadres – the men and women who will occupy key positions in the country, to promote its development by political leadership which is based on knowledge and training. The training of cadres is given more importance than the cultivation of scholarship for its own sake. In Bourguiba's words: 'The University's function is to train cadres, men destined to assume responsibilities at all levels of national life ...

to make a valid judgment on basic options and to play a useful part in State affairs.'

There are few other countries where a president has done so much to expound an ethos of society and government; none where a political leader has given so much time to praising civic and moral virtues, emphasizing the value of hard work, insisting that nationhood consists in the acceptance by citizens of their moral and civic responsibilities. What other president can say of himself: 'There was also Bourguiba. This young man with his faith and enthusiasm came to maturity from a somewhat agitated childhood and the course of history was changed,' and at the same time condemn mini-skirts, saying, 'When receiving women in audience I have frequently had to get them to sit beside me instead of in front of me, so as to avoid mutual embarrassment.'

What has been Bourguiba's impact on the Tunisian people? It has not been that of a charismatic leader who wields power through some kind of magical quality or who owes his authority to an emotional response from the populace. He is applauded without seeking to evoke the mass hysteria which crowds have shown in Nasser's Egypt. He is seldom praised beyond reason, and is bitterly attacked by only a few. It is easy to elicit, in conversation with Tunisians, both recognition of his virtues and criticism – whether he is reproached for undermining tradition or for insufficient radicalism.

The most significant aspect of his leadership has been that it is acceptable to the cadres of active, intelligent Tunisians holding important posts in the party. Such men share the fundamental assumptions of Bourguibism. They are convinced of the fragility and yet the potential of Tunisia; aware of the pitfalls into which a new nation (and old nations too) may fall, intent on the possibilities of development, conscious that such development can only come from the optimum input of hard work and well-conceived plans. Their conduct of government is very open – few developing countries can have been subjected to such close scrutiny by UN agencies, foreign governments, academic researchers and journalists; but they keep a fairly close society. They talk readily to foreigners but do not easily invite them into their homes; they give a strong impression of cohesion, in spite of evidence of predictable disagreement and diversity amongst themselves. They work hard, partly through commitment to what they are doing, partly because of the shortage of men in the great middle areas between top administrators and clerks.

Such men accept the need for stable government, and they respect Bourguiba for his past achievements. They accept his style. Men of government themselves, they believe in the authority of government; they also believe and have found that changes can be made most effectively if authority is combined with discussion, reasoning, argument and persuasion. Within a defined framework they exercise individual responsibility which permits a great deal of variety. They can claim to know their own colleagues and their own constituents and be able to represent their views and the possibilities of action to the central authority. They are not called on to undertake impossible tasks; they have found that small changes add up to major reforms and they are ready to learn from mistakes.

Without such men, as governors and delegates, party secretaries, members of party cells, undersecretaries in government departments, members of cultural committees in every major town, schoolteachers and local government officers, the Bourguiba ethos and leadership would be hollow.

At the same time ethos and leadership are not the sole components of Bourguiba's government. There is also authority, exercised with the arbitrariness of a prince. In a traditional Islamic society such authority is expected – it exists in the family, where it is sufficiently strong to be wielded by the oldest brother when the father is absent. As young people move into the modern world such authority may weaken, so that students in Tunis demonstrate on the streets – but at the same time other students, attending a summer course at Mahdia, readily accept that they may not leave their hostel at the weekend without producing the written consent of their father.

Bourguiba's authority has been widely accepted – it has been expected that those who challenge authority will be disciplined and brought to order. And Bourguiba has not hesitated to use his authority to counter any challenge to his leadership. On occasions he has harshly brushed aside the normal judicial process to act against those he believed might endanger his regime.

In 1958 ben Ammar, who had been prime minister in the Bey's government at the time of independence, was arraigned before the political High Court of Justice on charges of corruption. A special court was used in 1963 to condemn those held responsible for an attempt to assassinate him; five years later the group of intellectuals responsible for the *Perspectives tunisiennes* were condemned with a similar disregard for normal judicial rights. Like a prince, Bourguiba has conferred praise and honour – and, also like a prince, has jettisoned those who have become a political liability.

Bourguiba has thus safeguarded his own authority; but he has generally used it in a way that can be, and is, supported by reasoned argument. Freedom and participation in government have reached a higher level in Tunisia than in the rest of the Arab world, except in Lebanon; and in Tunisia they have been associated with a purpose-ful modernization which imposes a heavy strain on many citizens.

The question that remains is whether such conditions can survive the ageing of the President, and his eventual succession. The answer to that question will depend to some extent on the stability and the flexibility of the party organization he has created.

9   Party government

THE SOCIALIST DESTOUR PARTY was founded – under a different name, the Néo-Destour – to work for independence from
France. Since independence it has been the prime instrument of
government in a developing country.

Its role has been different from that of political parties in the
advanced countries of western Europe and America. It does not
exist as one party of several, serving the purpose of offering a choice
to the electorate. It is the only party – and has been since 1963, when
a small communist party was suppressed. It alone presents candidates to the electors. It does not step aside after an election, leaving
the work of legislation and administration to Ministers, an Assembly
and civil servants; it plays a central role in government, and its part
has increased at the expense of the non-party institutions.

The presupposition of its part in the government of the country
is not that it channels upwards the views of an electorate – although
it certainly does play this role. It is rather that independence is a
hard-won achievement, that development is still to be achieved,
and that the role of the party is to offer leadership in the movement
forward to economic improvement and independence and a
dignified standard of living for all Tunisians.

But as it does so it brings the country closer to a fundamental
dilemma. In many respects Tunisian development since independence has followed a 'westernizing' path. It is a path which leads
naturally to such essential features of a western political system as a
legal opposition, and toleration of political diversity. But neither the
Tunisian inheritance nor the political system of Tunisia has any

place for a democratic opposition; and when intellectual criticism was voiced in 1968 it was severely repressed.

An uneasy balance thus persists. Western values infused the movement for independence and now permeate the administration of the country. But those who would enjoy the full political and intellectual freedom of a western democracy risk severe penalties. The general political atmosphere remains freer than that of most political communities: but the fate of a few political prisoners is nonetheless harsh for that.

The possible sources of opposition in a newly independent Tunisia are easy to identify. One could expect that a party which was united in the pursuit of independence would be subject to increasing strains as self-government came nearer. Once independence is achieved, it is normal for a modernizing government to evoke opposition both from conservatives and from those who want to move faster. Personal rule excites personal rivalry and ambition. Groups which have played a key role in the struggle for independence, such as the trade unions, can be expected to cling to their autonomy and resist the dominance of a single party.

All these sources of opposition were present in Tunisia after independence, but they were either short-lived or fragmented. It was not necessary for the regime to maintain repressive measures or to establish the apparatus of a highly coercive state. The police were there to maintain public order rather than to spy on and control political opposition. The army was small. Those who quarrelled with the regime were generally outmanoeuvred – and then welcomed back to key positions, in a government which cannot afford to leave talent unexploited.

The most important exception to this generalization is in the career and death of Salah ben Youssef. In 1955 he held a position in the Néo-Destour movement rivalling that of Bourguiba, and he represented an alternative route which Tunisia might follow. Through predilection and through personal ambition he offered the option of an evocative Arab nationalism. He came out in open conflict with Bourguiba in 1955, when France offered something short of complete independence. Under an agreement which Bourguiba accepted Tunisia was to have control over its internal government, while a series of Conventions were to govern defence, foreign policy and schools (to ensure the rights of the French in Tunisia).

For Bourguiba the Conventions represented an important step towards independence, and one which he was prepared to accept in that sense. Salah ben Youssef took a more extreme position. He had just returned from Cairo, where he had been supported by the Egyptians as representing an independent Maghreb. He was able therefore to urge the rejection of the Conventions and to press for Tunisian support for an independent Maghreb – at a time when Morocco was still not independent and the Algerian revolt was at the end of its first year.

Bourguiba had insistently tried to achieve a reconciliation with ben Youssef. When this failed he succeeded in outmanoeuvring him – and in any case commanded the major forces of the Néo-Destour party; for all that ben Youssef had taken a leading part in organizing agricultural and other trade unions, the mass of the trade-union movement under Ahmed ben Salah supported Bourguiba. In October 1955 the Political Bureau of the Néo-Destour party expelled ben Youssef from the party: the following month its congress met – not in Tunis, but in Sfax, the one town where (it is said) if a Jerbian opens a grocer's shop two Sfaxians move in on either side to squeeze him out. The Congress gave overwhelming support to Bourguiba.

The struggle then moved into the country, and ben Youssef and his followers resorted to violence to recover their position. It looked as if urban terrorism and guerrilla fighting in the countryside would spread across the country – with the Youssefists getting assistance from Algeria. Fortunately the threat did not materialize on a large enough scale; if it had, the Tunisian government would not have had resources of its own to meet it and would have been caught between its extremist opponents and the French forces restoring order.

The visitor going to Tunis today has difficulty in visualizing a country on the brink of civil war. The experience was a traumatic one. It looked as if twenty years' work in the construction of a pragmatic party working through gradualist means and rational argumentation might collapse into the divisions which had formed so large a part of Tunisia's history. Instead the country was led by Bourguiba to independence, keeping important links with France. It followed this path while for a further seven years its neighbour Algeria fought a bitter war against the French and while Nasser rose to the height of his power in the aftermath of Suez. In the cause of its own peace, independence and development it cut itself off from the torrential mainstream of Arab nationalism. Salah ben Youssef fled and was condemned in his absence; in August 1961 he was assassinated.

It is difficult to predict what would have happened to Tunisian politics had Youssefism remained as an openly expressed alternative to Bourguiba's government, possibly organized in a second party – a state of affairs difficult to imagine in the turbulence of Arab politics, and even more with the Algerian conflict so close. As it is, the pan-Arab alternative to Bourguiba's moderate regime, closely linked to Europe and America, appears to retain little support. 'Imperialist domination' from the United States is not something which easily frightens Tunisians – any more than most Arabs were alive to a Russian threat when Britain tried to organize them into a Baghdad pact in the 1950's. Algeria is, if not a threat, a neighbour to be watched with caution, and Nasser's claims to speak for the Arabs are neither convincing nor impressive in their results – given that Bourguiba has got rid of the French as successfully as Nasser freed Egypt from the British. The instability of Syria, the strife of the Yemen, the harsh conflicts in independent Algeria make unity and economic development attractive for their own sake.

Radical nationalism is the new loyalty of the Arab world; Islam is its traditional faith. In opposition to the French, Bourguiba had accepted and preserved the customs of Islam as part of Arab and therefore Tunisian identity – while the French had taken care not to legislate against the tenets of religion. When independence was won, Bourguiba and the Néo-Destour took their stand on moderniz-ing principles which brought them into conflict with Islam, and they expropriated lands held by religious trusts (*habous*). Independence was immediately followed by the enactment of a code of personal statutes which abolished polygamy, made marriage a voluntary contract (rather than an agreement between families) and protected women by making divorce subject to judicial decision. One of the great Islamic universities, the Zitouna,[1] was incorporated into the University of Tunis as its theological faculty.

These changes, and the opposition which they provoked, had none of the character of a European battle against an established church. Islam has no organized establishment with the institutional strength of the Christian churches. The people are led in prayer by men whose devotion or voice and sense of poetry qualify them to do so, in the judgment of the faithful. The leadership of the community is provided by the *ulema*, the teachers and interpreters of the Koran. The Prophet inspired belief in a direct relationship between the faithful and God and, for whatever reason, religious leaders have never formed themselves into hierarchic institutions directing religious life – and disputing sovereignty with secular rulers.

Anticlericalism or its equivalent is therefore a rare phenomenon in the Islamic world – even in Kemalist Turkey and the Iran of the 'white revolution'. Nor has Bourguiba had any reason or motive to embark on an onslaught on Islam. The 1956 Tunisian constitution stated that 'the Tunisian State is free, independent, and sovereign. Islam is its religion and Arabic its language.' The absence of any sacerdotal priesthood makes it possible for Bourguiba and members of the Party to give the Friday sermon in mosques. Themselves devout in varying degrees, they use the opportunity which this offers to interpret Islam.

Arguments are not lacking to them. Nothing in the Prophet's teaching prescribes the veil; his precepts elevated the condition of women twelve hundred years ago and it is in the same spirit that their dignity is assured in the present; fasting, although one of the pillars of Islam, is not required in time of war – and Tunis is engaged in war against underdevelopment.

For all that it is impossible to seek to change habits consecrated by religion, to diminish the position of religious leaders and to re-distribute property held under religious law without encountering opposition. Such opposition has manifested itself most strongly over the Islamic month of fast, Ramadan. The stated grounds of Bourguiba's direct opposition to this central Muslim practice was that the country could not afford to have its working force made idle for a month during the fast – working short hours during the day and engaging in jollifications once the sun went down. But fasting, along with affirmation of belief, the giving of alms, prayer and pilgrimage are the five pillars of the faith. Fasting, like the observance of dietary prescriptions, has a self-sustaining tendency and becomes habitual – especially when the end of the fast is celebrated by a great feast and carnival. It is to be understood therefore that Bourguiba's attempt to end or at least attenuate observance of Ramadan should meet resistance, in the sense that Tunisians continued to fast, and provoke demonstrations of hostility as was the case in the holy city of Kairouan. The dispute was not clear-cut between the party and the religious leaders, for in some areas where the party is strong, notably Sousse, its members are also devout.

Kairouan was best able to lead in resisting change. The Islamic clock and calendar are related directly to the sun and the moon, so that the beginning and end of Ramadan must be determined by an authoritative observer (at a different time depending on the area of the world). The religious leaders in Kairouan met Bourguiba's attack on Ramadan at the end of 1960 therefore not only by maintaining the fast, but beginning and ending it one day after Bourguiba's prescribed date – in accordance with Cairo. They were followed by Sfax, thus dividing the loyalties of the Sfax party. At the beginning of the new year, in 1961, the government sought to weaken the Kairouan opposition by moving one of the leading Imams, a man who had been a director of the Zitouna and then made into a schoolteacher, to another post.[2] Mobs came out on the streets, the national guard were called out and a few citizens were killed. Rioting continued for twenty-four hours.

Thereafter the fervour of the attempt to end fasting died out, and it has generally been supposed that Bourguiba had failed. One might expect that as traditional ways are replaced by modern living in schools, universities, offices and factories the fast might disappear of itself. In 1966 the Swedish political scientist Lars Rudebeck carried out a survey amongst fifty-nine students in the Faculty of Sciences at the University of Tunis and established (for what such limited statistics are worth) that the parents of fifty-seven of the students observed Ramadan, while forty of the students themselves did.

Few Tunisians are deeply devout; but the practice of religion affects a wider area of daily behaviour than does Christianity in modern Europe or America. Where the regime has come into conflict with Islamic custom, therefore, the conflict has not been an ideological battle so much as an attempt to modify habits and codes of behaviour sanctified by religion and hallowed by long centuries of acceptance.

The party has turned the force of persuasion against religious practices which appear irrational on religious grounds. The party argues against the pilgrimage, on the grounds that it eats up the savings of poor families and uses foreign exchange. It disapproves of the practice of slaughtering a sheep for the feast, on the grounds that what was appropriate in a nomadic, desert society is un-necessary when there is a butcher in the village, and that Tunisia's stock of sheep can ill afford the wastage of festive slaughtering. But these are practices which, as well as being endowed with religious significance, bring change and variety into lives which otherwise are austere and unrelieved; they are not easily given up.

President and party not only seek to interpret Islam to suit the framework of a modern state. They continue religious observance (although Bourguiba is not thought by anyone to be devout and is believed by some to lack strong belief). The President has given money for the building of the Bourguiba mosque in his birthplace of Monastir, and the government pays for extensive restoration of Islamic monuments – the great mosque at Kairouan, the mosque at Mahdia, the *ribat* or monastic fortress at Monastir and that at Sousse. Projects of this sort form ideal public works programmes; they provide employment, give renewed elegance to ancient cities and a sense of local and religious pride.

Although resistance to religious change has been marked and opposition has flared into rioting in Kairouan, no formed opposition has emerged. Upper-class conservative religious leaders of the sort to be found in Tunis would have little following. At least for some they have the reputation of taking their religion lightly when it was a case of sipping an aperitif with the French in the days of the protectorate. They have little contact with the masses and no political party to offer. The fanaticism which has bound the Muslim Brothers together in Egypt and made them the most enduring and dangerous opposition to Nasser is not widespread in Tunisia. It seems to be the case therefore that the condemnation of the regime for practices contrary to religion which one can hear in Kairouan and elsewhere is not accompanied by the offer of a practical or attractive alternative to any large body of the population.

The institutional strength of Islam was not great in Tunisia, any more than elsewhere, and the resistance which the Bourguiba regime has met has been in habits and beliefs. It has been rather within the movement that institutional clashes have occurred. Part of the strength of the Néo-Destour in its opposition to the French lay in the trade-union movement. In part the movement had origins outside the party and grew up along with the organization of French workers in Tunisia. In part it was the creation of the Party, which saw the necessity and opportunity of organizing not only workers but small shopkeepers, both for its own sake and to oppose communist infiltration.

Two of the strongest personalities in the movement for independence made their career in the trade unions. The first was Ferhat Hached, who was responsible for leading the Tunisian unions away from the Confédération générale du travail at the end of the second world war (see p. 132). Hached's breakaway confederation, the UGTT, came to embrace all Muslim trade unionists before independence – and as a trade-union movement with international connections was safeguarded from repressive action similar to that which the French took against the Néo-Destour.

After Hached's murder (and an interval of nearly two years) he was succeeded by a second dynamic figure – Ahmed ben Salah. Ben Salah had been a schoolmaster, and his rise to prominence in the UGTT was in part accidental, in part because he recognized the possibilities which it offered to him. Hard-working and ambitious, he rapidly made a reputation for himself – of the sort that disquiets established leaders.[3] Moreover, he might not have become general secretary had not two possible successors, Habib Achour and Ahmed Tlili, been in prison when Hached was killed.

The result of Hached's work and ben Salah's leadership was that Tunisia moved into independence with a strong and vigorous trade-union movement, able to claim a part in the national struggle comparable in importance to the Néo-Destour itself, with a member-ship of 150,000 and a forceful young leader ready to make his mark on the new state. Ben Salah's policies differed from those of Bour-guiba in that he looked for radical economic reform and far-reaching measures of socialization. Whatever Bourguiba thought of a planned economy at this stage, the implementation of ben Salah's proposals would have meant the disruption of his gradualism and prejudiced a still delicate relationship with France. Moreover, ben Salah claimed a place for the trade-union movement (which he directed) equal with that of the party in the determination of economic policy – a claim which went far beyond those of most independent trade-union movements.

Such claims were unacceptable to the president and the party – and ben Salah's policies were rejected too. Unfortunately his position in the trade-union movement was insecure because of the rivalries he had excited. Habib Achour had been risking his life in a strike at Sfax in 1947 while ben Salah was still working for his degree in literature, and he it was who now, with the support of Bourguiba, led a breakaway from the UGTT. Shortly afterwards ben Salah was outflanked in the UGTT by the appointment of Ahmed Tlili as general secretary. Achour's new union (which was dis-tinguished simply by the omission of the word 'General' from its title – the UTT) was able, because of presidential and party backing, to bring about a reunion with the UGTT conditional on the expulsion of ben Salah and the ending of trade-union claims to government.

Ahmed ben Salah was left high and dry. But it is a significant fact of Tunisian political life that five years later, when Bourguiba modified his economic policies in the face of deepening economic stagnation and initiated the planning of the economy, he appointed Ahmed ben Salah to be director of planning – and ben Salah accepted. Apparently without recrimination he devoted his immense energies to a task equal to them, and became the second most important man in Tunisia.

Meanwhile the issue of what place a trade-union movement should have in the state had not been given final settlement. The Bourguiba government set about organizing state and society in an organic whole with exacting plans for economic development. Their instrument came to be increasingly the single party. The principal means of providing for investment was to keep wages stationary while prices rose – both gradually through an inflationary process and suddenly, in 1964, by devaluation of the currency. What, in this situation, could a trade-union movement do? Should it take its lead from the party and the government and use its influence with the workers to persuade them to accept changes which in the short run meant a rise in the cost of living, or should it follow traditional trade-union practice and defend its members' rights?

The response of the UGTT, still led by Habib Achour and Ahmed Tlili, was to insist that price rises consequent on devaluation should be accompanied by wage increases. Once again these trade unionists found themselves in conflict with Ahmed ben Salah – in reversed positions. It was now ben Salah who represented the power of the state and Achour who put forward the claims of an independent trade-union movement. The result was a drawn-out conflict in which the political leadership was again successful. Side issues arose to complicate the main battle. The UGTT had formed agricultural and fishing cooperatives; now the government was pressing forward with the promotion of its own cooperatives as the principal form of agricultural organization. It insisted that the existing UGTT cooperatives should be brought into the single general framework.

In the midst of the political struggle a ferry-boat running between Sfax and the Kerkenna islands caught fire and several people were drowned. The boat belonged to a UGTT cooperative of which Achour was manager, the appropriate fire regulations had not been complied with and the boat's insurance was not in order. Achour thereby became criminally liable and his parliamentary immunity was suspended. The position of the dissidents thus gravely weakened, Ahmed Tlili tried to win outside support by attending the congress of the International Confederation of Free Trade Unions in Amsterdam, in 1965. He tried but failed to secure recognition in place of the official delegation and brought his charges against his opponents before the world press – a rash gamble, since, when he failed, he could be reproached with wilfully besmirching the reputation of his colleagues in the eyes of outsiders.

By the end of July both Achour and Tlili had been defeated. A special Congress of the UGTT was held, and addressed by Bourguiba. In characteristic style Bourguiba paid tribute to the role of Achour and Tlili in the movement; but made clear that the UGTT should continue – as it had done before – to accept and support the government and the party in their economic policies. New statutes were framed and voted; a new Secretary-General was elected – Béchir Bellagha, who had a trade-union background but had recently been a regional governor. The Executive Bureau was also renewed.

Habib Achour was tried on charges relating to the boat and condemned to prison – but released shortly afterwards under amnesty. Ahmed Tlili remained in exile until the spring of 1967 when he returned, a sick man, to die shortly afterwards. Before his death he expressed his reconciliation with Bourguiba.

The trade-union organization is not the only one which has been brought into line with the party and under its control. The Néo-Destour movement owed much to the student world of Tunisia, to the scholars who won their way to Sadiki College and then went on to study in Paris. They have their successors in the University of Tunis and at Paris now. In Tunis, students may join the Union Générale des Etudiants Tunisiens, or they may join the party and become members of the Fédération Nationale des Etudiants Destouriens.

Students, of all people, do not take easily to permeation by an organization of the Destourian kind. In 1967 students scarcely remembered the protectorate; for them, authority is represented by the Tunisian state and the authority of the party. They claim the right to organize their own affairs, and resent the privileges of the Destourian students. They welcome the UGET, but would wish to elect its own officers freely, however critical they may be of the regime. It was these emotions which exploded in demonstrations and fighting which broke out in December 1966. The sparking point was an insignificant incident in a bus, but the consequent disturbance was sufficient for nine students to be arrested, and for some of them to be given suspended sentences. *L'Action*, the party newspaper, made believe that irresponsible elements had exploited an incident; but the independent *Jeune Afrique* was undoubtedly nearer the truth when it wrote: 'Last week in Tunis, impatience and passion were expressed, not revolt.'[4]

The outcome of the disturbance was that the Party remained in control of the student organization; students expected that if they elected officers to UGET who were critical of the Destourian party they would be deprived of any influence.

The political life of Tunisia has thus been punctuated by conflicts which have left the Party in a dominant position. The history of the newspaper press has followed a similar course. The newspaper *L'Action* was closed in 1958 after its criticism of the trial of Ben Ammar. The two men held most responsible – Mohamed Masmoudi and the editor, Beshir ben Yahmed – came under severe censure. (Masmoudi was expelled from the Political Bureau.) They suffered the same fate three years later when *Afrique-Action* criticized personal regimes in general and (implicitly) Bourguiba in particular. Subsequently Masmoudi came back into favour and was reappointed to the Paris Embassy, while ben Yahmed left Tunisia to become editor of *Jeune Afrique*, a successor to *Afrique-Action*.

The press was the poorer as a result. In addition to the French and Arabic party press (*L'Action*, founded in 1962, and *Al Amal*), a few independent newspapers remained. One of them, *La Presse*, was taken over by the government in 1967 and its editor charged with currency offences. They are careful to keep within the bounds of acceptable criticism. Meanwhile, the foreign press is readily available and *Le Monde* is followed by a small readership throughout the country.

But the strength of president and party in the country is not attributable solely to the negative aspects of the containment of opposition. In the last resort much is attributable to the record and the position of Bourguiba himself. He has been the object of an attempted assassination. But except for a small minority – and a minority which in recent years has diminished rather than grown – Tunisia without Bourguiba is difficult to imagine, and the success of the president gives him great reserves of credit. When the authority of Bourguiba is involved there will inevitably be important groups of key men who will believe that he has been right often enough in the past in his calculation of tactics and strategy for it to be likely that he is right again; and even if he is not, his authority must nevertheless stand. He is not vindictive, and the examples of ben Salah, put in his place in 1956 and returning to power in 1961, or of Mohamed Masmoudi, are characteristic of the regime.

In addition, the authority of the party always receives support from those who can see the danger that Tunisia may collapse into disunion and even civil strife. The danger of violence is difficult to judge; the calm rationality of some Tunisians, the docility of the majority in the face of authority suggest that such discord is a remote possibility. But the history of the country has its share of violence; the experience of Youssefism is very close, the example of other Arab states is always present. In June 1967 crowds emerged from the medina and burned the British Embassy, stoned the United States information centre, set fire to American cars, Jewish shops and the synagogues. Bourguiba is a safeguard against chaos, and there are many who follow his judgment in the construction of a new country rather than risk conflict and civil strife.

In addition, government, party and president in Tunisia remain uncorrupt. No political scientist has given an adequate explanation of what makes for purity and what creates corruption in society, and one cannot do better than to state that by any standards Tunisia is uncorrupt. Corruption may be financial or it may be political – it may be corruption by money or corruption by power. Neither exists in Tunisia in any significant degree. This is not to say that influence and wealth never count for anything. But they do not count for more, and probably less, than in most other countries. Officials and party militants do not cling to office for the bribes and perquisites it provides; they do not wield power solely for the satisfaction it gives, nor diminish others for their own self-aggrandisement – at least no more than the imperfections of human nature make inevitable. Bourguiba, it is true, enjoys wealth and splendour appropriate to a monarch; but he does not amass wealth in the style of some parvenu rulers. His authority and that of the Destourians undoubtedly owes much to political purity.

Moreover, party and government have been able to renew themselves; the supreme combatant remains, but new and young men fill party offices and government posts.

The fact remains that the political history of Tunisia since independence has been of the concentration of power in the party, and its streamlining and development as the motive force of the state. At the time of independence the Néo-Destour had no serious rival; but there were a small communist party, groups of independents, the national organizations like the trade-union movement and the farmers' unions. It had been taken for granted in the struggle for independence that the form of government would follow an established western pattern, with a popularly elected assembly and a government related to it. In 1956 such an assembly was elected, with the first task of drawing up a constitution.

Under Bourguiba's direction the electoral law for the choosing of this Assembly was drawn on a majority basis. Parties prepared lists of candidates, and the party winning a constituency took the seats belonging to it. The law offended the views of some liberal members of the party; but it ensured that the Néo-Destour sub-merged even such organized opposition as was to be found. At the same time the drawing up of party lists provided for the dominance of leadership within the party. The achievement of the opposition was thus insignificant – although some 71 per cent of the electorate abstained in Youssefist Jerba and 41 per cent in Tunis.[5]

At this time Tunisia was not yet a republic – the Bey retained his position and prerogatives, and Bourguiba was prime minister. It might have been expected that the first task of the newly independent country would be to draw up a new constitution. But Bourguiba saw that the practice of government must be established before a new constitution was promulgated – lest the constitution should limit excessively the power and flexibility of the government. The drafting of the constitution was, therefore, not completed until 1959. In the meantime the Bey was deposed, and Bourguiba became president. He took over the Bey's prerogative powers – on which he had already relied as prime minister. The government remained independent of the Assembly in the sense that it did not require approval of the budget, kept priority for the government's business in the timetable and so greatly attenuated the right of private members to introduce bills; and in any case could legislate by decree.

The pattern of the Assembly was thus established, confirmed in the constitution of 1959 – and remains the same today. It meets for short periods, and has no effective power. It is used as a means of giving dignity and importance to its members, to act as a sounding board for the president and to provide discussion and elucidation of the government's policies.

While the Assembly was given this minor role, the government, under Bourguiba's direction, retained power. A similar and comparable process was undertaken in the party. During the fight for independence the party had retained a considerable amount of decentralization, as was appropriate to the political conditions in which it operated. The mild repression of the French was much less than the police rule of a despotism, so that there was no need for a highly disciplined revolutionary body of a Leninist kind; and at the same time it was essential to maintain local commitment, and the continuance of local organization while the national leadership was in prison or exile. In addition, the coming of independence had led to a rapid rise in the membership of the party as thousands of Tunisians rushed to join the winning side.

In 1958 Bourguiba reformed the party in a centralizing manner. The councils of regional federations, which had been elected from branches, were ended, and party commissioners appointed in their place. The National Council of the party was given a new importance on paper but in fact was not summoned. A single party congress was held in the eight years from 1956 to 1964.

Within three years of independence the structure of government thus consisted of a formal apparatus like that of a western European country, parallel with a party organization – with power concentrated at the top, in Bourguiba's hands. Bourguiba's lieutenants were ministers and members of a Cabinet Council in the formal structure of government, and they composed the political bureau of the party. Ahmed ben Salah, Mohamed Masmoudi, Ahmed Mestiri, Mongi Slim, Ahmed Tlili, Hedi Nouira and the general secretary Bahi Ladgham were amongst those who composed the fifteen-man membership of the Political Bureau in these early days. They included all the important members of the leadership; but they did not wield power independently of Bourguiba, who retained control of decisions and policy. The parallel structure of government and party was extended to each of fourteen governorates, each with a governor and a party commissioner. The number of party branches was reduced, so that there was one for each local government area or *sheikhat*.

In 1964 a further change in the formal structure of party and state was adopted by a Party Congress, known as the 'Congress of Destiny' – a suitable sequel to the 'Congress of Victory' of 1959. Destiny was now in the hands of the Tunisian people. They were completely sovereign now that the evacuation of all foreign troops and the nationalization of colonized land were complete. They were to grasp this destiny by driving towards economic and social development, using the means of Tunisian socialism to these ends. From now on, the party itself was known as the Socialist Destourian Party.

The Congress played an important part in the political life of the nation. It was attended by some 1,300 delegates – a large number in proportion to the educated cadres of the nation. Its importance was to confirm the constitutional development of the country in the way it was going rather than to make a fundamental new departure. The fusion of the national government and the party was carried a step further. All secretaries of state were made members of the central committee of the party; so were all governors (the number of governorates being reduced to thirteen). The President of the Republic naturally remained president of the party, and the leading ministers were members of the political bureau.

The most important aspect of the changes introduced by the Congress of Destiny was, however, that which concerned regional government. From now on there were to be two key men in each governorate – the governor and the party secretary. The former continued to be appointed as the agent of the national government, exercising executive and administrative functions, with wide-ranging authority for the area under his control. The party secretary is chosen through the party machinery. He works in close co-operation with the governor, and it has generally been possible to pair two men who complement each other – so that, for example, at least one of the two has received higher education. The task of the party secretary is to maintain contact with the party leadership and members throughout the governorate.

Governors and party secretaries are supported in their task by committees of co-ordination – one in each governorate, elected by a regional congress to which party branches send delegates. Election follows the normal process of nomination, encouragement and dis-couragement. The only way in which a would-be member of a committee of co-ordination can present himself as a candidate is by making himself known and acceptable to party officials. The governor and the party secretary will then encourage some men – probably younger educated persons – and discourage some of the older militants who may be thought out of tune with the new needs of the party and government. Although care is thus taken to ensure that selection is made from the right people, an important element of choice nonetheless remains. The elections of the first committees of co-ordination in August 1965 involved the free choice, by the delegates at the party congress, of some ten to twenty members of each committee from roughly twice that number of candidates.[6]

In common with other Tunisian institutions (except the Presidency) the party has thus been subject to change in the pursuit of its most effective role. There can be no doubt that it has succeeded in establishing itself as a powerful instrument of political mobilization. It is unchallenged by any other organization in the country and its members animate and direct the national organizations – the trade union movement, the student organizations and the National Union of Tunisian Women. It has been able to renew itself and is not dominated by the old combatants. From being a party of the struggle for independence it has transformed itself into a party of government. It is at the centre of a political process by which new men are selected and encouraged to take on responsibilities in the party. It relies on the traditional practice of Arab society by which notables come to be known to an electing body and thus receive their votes; but it has also succeeded in establishing a genuine element of electoral choice.

The base of the party as well as its cadres has been expanded by the recruitment of new men. In the villages, party officials are recruited through the committees of co-ordination, and serve as officials because it gives them prestige in the village. A successful branch officer finds employment for the men of the village, who then become members of the party and pay dues.[7] At the same time, the party is welded to the traditional life of the village. The ritual of party celebration is superimposed on more traditional rites; in the village of Sidi Ameur, national days – Martyrs' Day (9th April), the day of Bourguiba's return from exile after independence (1st June) – are celebrated by a party meeting at the *hadra*, with music from Tunisian folklore musicians.

Through the party, the president and government of the country thus have indirect access to the people as a whole. The purpose of such access is not to give villagers or workers in the towns a free choice between alternative programmes of government. It is rather to change traditional practices into modern methods of cultivation and production, to instil a slow ferment into the accepted order of society, to promote change through education, understanding and rational argument.

The task is in no way easy. To take one example, the govern-ment's policy is to reduce the number of olive trees and to improve the productivity of those that remain. It draws on the resources of foreign aid and technical skill to replace olive trees with others whose fruit can be exported to earn foreign exchange, and it seeks to make a cash crop of olive oil. But in the north and in the Sahel, the olive tree is far more than a mere producer of olives and oil. It is an essential element of security. Trees are bought and sold as men are well off or fall on more difficult times. The oil has a wide range of uses, from nourishment to cosmetic; the pruned branches are used for fuel. The olive tree is spoken of as 'praising God', and the apricot considered useless. The village women have no wish to earn cash to buy oil in the town, for they regard it (no doubt rightly) as inferior to what they make themselves.

The villagers do not very readily rebel or resort to violence to sabotage the government's programmes; they belong to an old society in which authority has long been respected, and do what the government says. But to that extent the party has only succeeded in half its task. Its essential role is not only to promote economic development, but to invoke the active participation of the people.

10   Tunisia in the modern world

A NATION DERIVES its sense of cohesion from language, history – a sense of past glory and of future possibilities. But it also derives an identity from the place it occupies in the world. It may seem that foreign-policy questions are of minimal importance to men whose primary concern is with gaining a livelihood – and this is borne out by the lack of interest which a modern electorate shows in external affairs. Nevertheless ordinary citizens are influenced in their behaviour and outlook by the position which they think the nation holds in the eyes of others – the role it plays and the reputation it enjoys. Of this European nations, which have seen surges or decline and renewed pre-eminence, are well aware.

Independence for some new states has presented leaders with the opportunity to cut a figure in world politics and to make a bid for leadership for the area or the group of peoples whom they can claim to represent. Others, like Tito, have had a position of outstanding importance thrust upon them.

Tunisia has made no such bid for the heady heights of leadership. Under Bourguiba's direction it has pursued a modest role in world affairs, avoiding dangers which have beset it from its neighbours and retaining its security. Such a course has sometimes called for much political skill, and Bourguiba has shown himself adept at using words which appear to give Tunisia importance as a sage and wise counsellor in the affairs of the world and its most immediate neighbours, without involving any major commitments of prestige or armaments. The one exception to this prevailing pattern was the initiative which he took with regard to the French maintenance of the Bizerte base in 1961.

The countries of outstanding importance to Tunisia might be thought to be its neighbours of the Maghreb – though in fact relations between the countries of north-west Africa are not close – and France. Tunisia also belongs to the Arab world; it has established a valuable relationship with the United States, the source of a major part of aid coming from abroad, but has been eclectic in its choice of relationships. It has avoided any commitment to the Soviet bloc, even of the sort which so often goes under the title of neutralism, but has assistance agreements with several of them.

In many respects the countries of the Maghreb may be thought to form a natural unit and it might be expected that relations between them would rapidly grow very close. But the history of the area suggests no reason why this should be the case. A united Maghreb has only enjoyed the most ephemeral existence. Ifriqiya and Morocco can claim the longest identity and stability as virtually independent political units; between them Algeria for long periods of its history was a territory which was attached in parts of differing size and importance to its neighbours. To the east Ifriqiya embraced part of modern Libya; but although Tunis and Tripoli were for long periods under the same ruler they did not form any close union, and the desert was a barrier between them.

Nor did French colonial rule make for a greater unification. North African students, it is true, met in Paris and formed ideas and plans together for independence. But the history of French rule was of division between the territories, of a relationship between each of them and Paris rather than of a force to draw them together. The occupation of Algeria was the oldest, and the northern part of Algeria was integrated into France, forming overseas departments which sent deputies to the French National Assembly. Tunisia never gained the same importance as a French colony as Algeria and continued to be administered formally as a protectorate. The centralized administration of France and its empire provided no incentive to draw together three territories which had come under French rule at widely differing periods of time.

The common pattern and the common language which French rule imposed on the three countries of the north-west was thus of limited importance. Libya was subjected to the quite different experience of Italian colonization. Moreover, the struggle for independence differed between all four countries, not least between those under French rule, and the shape of politics and culture which emerged therefore varied deeply. This has been especially true of Tunisia and its neighbour Algeria. For Tunisia the battle for independence was relatively calm, and involved (in comparison with the Algerian war) little bloodshed or violence. Possibly as a result Tunisia has asserted again and again its independence from France and has developed its economy through a close relationship with the United States. In Algeria, by contrast, France is the western power most accepted, the country to which Algerians feel the closest attachment outside the Arab world – the country with which indeed the closest attachment exists, if it is measured by the half-million or more Algerian workers in France (the number having increased since independence).

Tunisia, Algeria and Morocco have thus succeeded in establishing three different types of political structure – Tunisia a stable moderate republic, Algeria having gone through the common Arab experience of a military coup, Morocco a relatively conservative monarchy. In most important respects Tunisia is more advanced and progressive than Algeria. Nowhere is this more true than in the position of women, which has scarcely changed in Algeria while young Tunisians are increasingly emancipated. In agricultural development and effective economic planning Algeria lags behind Tunisia, while laying claim nonetheless to be amongst the progressive Arab states.

It was this commitment to radicalism on the part of Algeria's revolutionary leaders which made most difficult the relations between it and Tunisia. When Salah ben Youssef attacked Bourguiba for his acceptance of the agreements with France in 1955 he had the support of the Algerians. An alliance existed between the FLN in Algeria and the Egyptian government, and it was in Algerian interests to have a Tunisian leader geographically in the middle of similar political disposition. Such an ally in Tunisia would greatly facilitate the despatch of arms from Egypt to Algeria (traffic which in addition went by sea, leading to the capture of an arms shipment by the French in 1956).

The conflict between Tunisia and the provisional Algerian government continued throughout the war, as the Youssefists received support from the Algerian National Liberation Army – and the dispute overlapped with Tunisia's quarrel with Egypt for its support and sheltering of ben Youssef. When independence came to Algeria it appeared that the tables might be turned when Bourguiba supported ben Bella's rival ben Khedda, but in fact such interference never became serious. It was eclipsed in the year of Algerian independence by the implication of Youssefists in the plot to assassinate Bourguiba in December 1962, which once again brought relations with Algeria to a low ebb.

Throughout these early years the relationship between the two countries can be seen as a continuation of earlier history – of the interference of neighbouring kingdoms in each other's affairs in the pursuit of political advantage. The modern element was in the different political and personal position of Bourguiba and ben Bella – the former a moderate gradualist leader whose power derived from a well-articulated party organization, the latter a combative revolutionary relying to a large extent on a generalized appeal to the people (which subsequently proved too weak to survive a military plot).

Morocco is more distant from Tunisia, frontier disputes are impossible and mutual interference unlikely. Nor has Morocco sought to embrace Tunisia in some major concerted campaign or collective action towards Arab unity. The experience of the two countries in the pursuit of their own independence had more in common than either had with Algeria. It is not surprising that exactly a year after the independence of the two countries – in March 1957 – Bourguiba should pay an official visit to Morocco ending in the signature of a treaty of friendship between the two countries.

Three years later, however, Morocco recalled its Ambassador from Tunis in protest against the latter's recognition of the state of Mauritania. This new republic is unlikely ever to become a major power in world affairs – its territory is largely desert and its natural resources few; but Morocco's claims on it were sufficient to determine briefly the alignment of African states, so that Egypt and Mali joined in an unnatural alliance with Morocco and were known as the Casablanca group.

Meanwhile relations between Algeria and Morocco were much worse than those between Morocco and Tunis, since they turned on territorial claims which Morocco made on Algeria, not for barren sands, but for the highly important area of Tindouf, rich in iron ore. Algerian possession of Tindouf, in the extreme west of the territory – nearly a thousand miles from Algiers and less than five hundred from Casablanca – follows from the earlier French occupation of Algeria and the extension of French rule across the desert to the south of the kingdom of Morocco. Historical accident, however, is unlikely to remove or to compromise rival claims on rich territory. True, the Algerian government made a verbal concession to Morocco in the heyday of the Casablanca alliance: a convention was signed between King Hassan II and Ferhat Abbas (as President of the Algerian provisional government) in which the Algerian government recognized 'the territorial problem posed by the delimitation imposed arbitrarily by France between the two countries'. But Algerian independence was accompanied by bloodshed at Tindouf as the Algerians took over from the French army. Thereafter the divergence between the political regimes of the two countries became increasingly apparent, Algeria received military aid from Egypt and frontier incidents multiplied.

Political differences, the existence of political forces which overlap state boundaries and frontier disputes, thus created major obstacles to common action between the former French territories of northwest Africa, quite apart from the possible fourth partner, Libya. Even when common opposition to France was strongest it did not lead to a permanent alliance between the Maghreb countries. On one notorious occasion, in October 1956, a Maghreb conference was forestalled by the action of the French authorities in ordering down to Algiers the aeroplane carrying ben Bella and four other Algerian leaders from Rabat to Tunis. But in spite of such incidents none of the three Maghreb countries could see greater advantages for itself in union with the other two than in the maintenance of at least satisfactory relations with France.

The result has been an extremely slow and limited growth of co-operation within the Maghreb, in spite of the obvious advantages which such development has to offer. To some extent this is attributable to the common fact that states involved in a rapid transformation of their own society adopt an isolationist posture and are reluctant to jeopardize the reform of their own structures by attempts at co-ordination with others – as the United States rejected a World Economic Conference in favour of the New Deal and the British Labour government was reluctant to join a European com-munity at the time of its own institutional and economic reform.

The economic advantages of co-operation are obvious, and were explored by a committee of the United Nations Economic Com-mission for Africa. Its report – the Ewing report – was concerned with problems of industrialization, and made recommendations for a co-ordinated plan for the development of energy (based on the Algerian resources of natural gas) for the exploitation and conversion of phosphates and the development of other industries including metallurgy, glass, cement and textiles. Other areas in which one might expect consultation to be effective are in the export and marketing of primary products, such as olives and olive oil, in which the three countries compete with each other.

The Ewing report gave the necessary stimulus to a series of conferences in 1964, under the aegis of the UN Economic Com-mission for Africa. As a result, the decision was taken, at the Tangiers conference of November 1964, to establish two permanent institutions for economic co-operation – a Centre of Industrial Studies at Tripoli, financed by the Special Fund of the UN, and a permanent Consultative Committee.

There was, however, very little momentum following this im-portant step forward. Arrangements were made for co-ordination in the export of alfafa, and the Consultative Committee met inter-mittently at Algiers. But nothing was done to reduce tariff duties between the Maghreb countries, far less to co-ordinate investment or to extend co-ordination of exports. Each country continued to make commercial agreements independently; Algeria in 1965 signed an important agreement on oil with France; the three countries continued separate negotiations with the European Common Market.

Only in 1967 did it seem that fresh impetus was being given to the weak institutions of co-operation. A conference meeting at Tunis in November took up proposals of the Permanent Committee. The conference devised an agreement for the reduction and elimina/tion of tariff and quantitative restrictions on lists of industrial products, to be brought into force over a period of five years. It also made provision for consultation when any one of the four countries carried out industrial investment, in the hope of arriving at an agreement on the elimination of customs duties and the establish/ment of a common external tariff.

The practical outcome of these prolonged and intermittent attempts to reach an effective agreement was limited in scope. Tunisians discussing the economic development of their country have always laid stress on the importance of Maghreb unity; but without being able to achieve very striking results in practice. To some extent the need for each of the Maghreb countries to negotiate with the European Economic Community has assisted co-operation between them. Here too the starting-point was one of wide differences between Algeria and the other states, since Algeria was part of France when the Rome Treaty was signed and was expressly provided for under article 227 of the Treaty. The Community itself has not undertaken a vigorous policy of actively encouraging economic integration in the Maghreb (as the United States did towards Europe under the Marshall plan). It has confined itself to considering the problems of separate states, and it has inevitably encouraged those states to look at their problems as a whole. But for Tunisia trade with France and Europe far exceeds that with the Maghreb. It has, therefore, persistently sought to improve its standing with the Community and vigorously pursued the objective of Associate status.

The attempt to bring about co-operation between the countries of the Maghreb must be set against the background of their limited commercial exchanges, which are on a very small scale compared with trade with the rest of the world. Figures of imports and exports of the three former French territories show that Tunisia alone sent anything like a significant percentage of its exports to the other countries of the Maghreb – less than 8 per cent. Tunisian imports from Morocco and Algeria amounted to only 2 per cent of total imports. For Algeria and Morocco the percentage of both imports and exports to the rest of the Maghreb is less than 2.5 per cent of the total for the world. For Libya the figures are even lower.[1] Understandably France remains the biggest supplier and market for the three western countries; Italy the foremost supplier of Libya, although lagging behind Britain and the German Federal Republic as a market.

Not least striking in the state of trade between the North African countries is the fact that Algeria supplied oil only to Morocco, and (in 1966) came third after the Soviet Union (supplying twice as much as Libya) and Saudi Arabia. Libya supplied oil to Tunisia (but not to Morocco) for refinement at Bizerte – although in 1965 Tunisia bought more crude oil from Iran (277,000 tons) than from Libya (260,000 tons).

Tunisia may be seen as belonging not only to the Maghreb and the Arab east, but to the continent of Africa. Yet the whole history of the country shows how much less important this connection has been than that with the Islamic world and with Europe. The Sahara is a more formidable barrier than the Mediterranean. There have always been trading links across the desert, but they have not been close; nor has there been the same intermingling of peoples from north and south in Tunisia as there has been in southern Morocco. The Islamic world extends round the Sahara into central Africa; but there are no close religious ties across the desert; Kano and Tunis both have a link to Mecca, but not to each other.

The Tunisian government has nonetheless participated actively in the affairs of the continent, to the extent that the condition of African politics makes possible. It has a commitment and sense of identity with the 'third world', and the African states are its near neighbours. But it has no ideology which it wishes to propagate in Africa, and no disputes of its own in which it looks for African support (except for the Bizerte crisis).

Tunisia has given support to the independence movement of Angola; Holden Roberto is the only nationalist leader to have an office in Tunis. But in other key disputes – such as Rhodesia – Bourguiba's policy has been as moderate as one would predict. His government has tried to mediate in the disputes of others – between Morocco and Mauritania, Ethiopia and Somalia. This policy of mediation and moderation has been surrounded with the Bourguibist ethos of moving forward by stages – to independence, then development and unity, the three necessary stages in man's eternal struggle for dignity. Inevitably relations have been closest with states most sympathetic to such a view of the world, Senegal chief amongst them.

Although Tunisia's relations with the other countries of the Maghreb have not been as close as one might at first expect, they inevitably had an important effect in the early years of Tunisian independence on relations with France, as long as the Algerian war continued. In those years Bourguiba trod an uneasy path between the FLN in Algeria and the French government. The acceptance of the conventions of 1955 implied an alliance with liberal forces in France against the Youssefists, with their supporters in Algeria; on the other hand the common cause of North African independence linked Tunisia to the Algerian nationalist movement in an alliance which the Tunisians would not sacrifice for the sake of commercial agreements with France. For similar reasons they sought a supply of arms from Britain and the United States rather than being dependent on France.

Tunisia suffered from the war with Algeria – as when French planes bombed the village of Sakiet Sidi Youssef in February 1958. The assertion of Tunisian independence led to minor conflicts of prestige with the French, as when they were provoked into the recall of their ambassador by the Tunisians bulldozing down a wall of the ambassador's residence for road improvement. (The residence had been that of the Resident-General and was proportionately large and prestigious.) It was in Bourguiba's interest, therefore, to act as mediator whenever opportunity presented itself. In the spring of 1961 he met de Gaulle at Rambouillet and it appeared that substantial progress was being made towards an Algerian settlement and in French relations with Tunisia.

But this was followed by the first major clash with France since independence when Bourguiba precipitated a crisis with France over the French base at Bizerte. There seems little doubt that development of events did not follow his intentions. The Bizerte base was the only remaining French military establishment in Tunisia, and previous negotiations – including the Rambouillet meeting – gave every reason to expect that it would be evacuated. But in July Bourguiba sent a letter to de Gaulle accusing France of extending the airfield and insisting on a definite timetable for the evacuation of the base. At the same time a claim was made for a small area of the Sahara in territory which would become Algerian.

Bourguiba appears to have intended that his provocative diplomatic action should be backed up by demonstrations and political action – while at the same time Tunisian troops were sent to the disputed frontier area. But fighting broke out in Bizerte – started it seems by the action of Tunisians in firing on a French helicopter. The French reaction was extremely vigorous and the Tunisians had little defence to offer against French armaments. The Tunisian government took the case to the United Nations where it won widespread support: the UAR and Liberia introduced a resolution calling for a cease-fire and negotiations for evacuation of the base, although they had to compromise with a more limited British and American resolution to secure unanimity. Meanwhile the French action at Bizerte had been disproportionately harsh (in the judgment of foreign observers) and had caused casualties numbered in thousands.

Whatever Bourguiba's intentions at the opening of the Bizerte crisis he drew the maximum political advantage from it. When the battle died down his position was very weak – French troops were in possession of Bizerte, support from the west was only moderate (for Britain and America the Berlin wall was far more important than Tunisia) and the backing of the Arab League was noisy without being very effective. As a first step Bourguiba therefore seized on the slightest opening in de Gaulle's position to take up negotiations, with the result that French troops were withdrawn from the town, and, at the end of the year, talks were renewed which eventually led to the evacuation of the base.

At the same time Bourguiba developed the improved relations which had been established with the Arab Middle East. The most important aspect of this improved relationship followed fast on the Bizerte battle – Salah ben Youssef was assassinated in August 1961, some say on orders from Bourguiba, and when Egyptian support had been withdrawn from him. Youssefism did not disappear altogether from Tunisia – it contributed to the plot from which Bourguiba escaped so narrowly in December 1962 – but its importance dwindled rapidly.

Meanwhile Tunisian relations with Egypt continued to grow closer. Visits were exchanged and commercial agreements signed in the spring of 1962; a fresh reconciliation occurred after the assassination attempt – Bourguiba took advantage of the conference of African states in Addis Ababa in March 1963 for this purpose. Above all the evacuation of the Bizerte base provided the opportunity for great manifestations of unity between Tunisia, Egypt and Algeria – but not Morocco, since the Tindouf dispute was at its height. Brave words were spoken and the political differences of the past were buried. Bourguiba claimed to have done more in an hour's conversation with ben Bella than in twenty years of diplomatic negotiations and to have had a fruitful interview with Nasser. 'Bizerte will, I hope, have brought a substantial contribution to the rapprochement of the Maghrebin and Arab peoples.'

At the same time the evacuation of the base was evidence of a stable relationship with France which had accompanied the rapprochement with Egypt. In 1962 and 1963 important agreements were signed between the two countries. An agreement of March 1963 provided for the Tunisian government to take over land from French settlers, with arrangements for compensation paid by the Tunisian government. In August of the same year agreements were signed covering the protection of French investments and Frenchmen working in Tunisia, providing a French loan, and dealing with the status of Tunisian workers in France. At the beginning of the new year, in 1964, fresh agreements were signed by which France contributed a loan to help finance Tunisian development and extended its commercial agreements.

Only a few months later the Tunisian government brusquely interrupted the smooth course of its relations with France by nationalizing the remainder of foreign land holding in Tunisia – a total of 300,000 hectares, of which four-fifths belonged to French-men. (Of the remainder the major part belonged to Italians, some 8,000 hectares to Maltese and something over a thousand to Swiss.)

The decision was presented by Bourguiba in a dramatic speech in which he said that the foreign possession of land was a 'question of life and death' for Tunisia. He denied that the new law was enacted in any spirit of vengeance towards the French *colons*; but at the same time presented their ownership of Tunisian land as a threat to sovereignty. France, he said, was in a position to indemnify the *colons*, who should be pleased that they were not called to account for eighty-three years of exploitation.

In view of the fact that previous agreements had been satisfactorily negotiated with France for the expropriation of French lands – and in view of the administrative difficulties which the new law created for Tunisians in making effective administrative arrangements for providing skilled men to take over the management and cultivation of new land – it must be assumed that the motives for the nationaliza-tion were political. It has been said that Bourguiba's objective was to give satisfaction to his critics within the country and to make Tunisia respectable in the eyes of the radical Arab states, with which relations were still unusually close. A more long-term political objective, however, must have been to subordinate French property to the same over-all direction as Tunisian. Since 1961 economic policy had been directed towards a planned economy and the development of larger units of production and exchange. It was a programme fraught with difficulty, but the obstacles would only have been greater had a private (and prosperous) sector remained in the hands of the former colonists.

The price which Tunisia had to pay for the nationalization was high since the French reaction was sharp – as previous experience of Gaullist government would lead one to expect (although it seems to have taken the Tunisians by surprise). The new law was voted on 11 May; two days later the French government cancelled a loan of 45 million francs and reduced its aid to industrial projects; it suspended an enlarged programme of technical assistance and recalled some sixty experts working with the Tunisian Ministry of Agriculture. In June it cancelled a commercial agreement, of which the most important part was provision for the import of Tunisian wine into France, for the most part free of duty, the remainder at half the normal duty.

But however nationalist and political Tunisian action may have been, it did not draw the country into an exclusive alliance with other Arab states or with the Soviet Union. From the days before independence, good relations had existed with the United States and these had developed to the material benefit of Tunisia.

The landing of American troops in North Africa in the second world war had shown Bourguiba the advantage which could be taken of an American relationship. In June 1943 he had sought American support, through the U.S. Consul Doolittle, against the repression by the French of the Néo-Destour movement. In 1946 and again in 1951 he went to the United States to press the Tunisian case for independence. The relations which the Tunisian trade-union movement established with the AFL at this time were to be of major importance in the development of the American programme in aid of Tunisia.

Independence was followed by mutual diplomatic support. The United States was the first great power to recognize the new state. A year later Eisenhower offered support, in the Eisenhower doctrine, to Middle Eastern states in danger from communism – an offer which received scant welcome in the Middle East, except in Lebanon and Iraq, and which was generally regarded as maladroit. But Bourguiba announced that 'the interest of Tunisia is to adhere to the new American policy'. In 1958 he refused to view the landing of American troops in Lebanon as 'colonialist'. 'The United States', he said, 'has no expansionist aims and no comparison can reasonably be established between American intervention in Lebanon and Soviet intervention in Hungary.'

Meanwhile, American aid had begun to flow into Tunisia in an expanding stream. Aid to the value of 18 million dollars in 1957 grew to 57 million in 1960. The following year it was yet more important. The United States made massive provision of wheat to counter the effects of a major drought. But of more long/term significance was the fact that Tunisia moved to a planned economy at the moment when the United States government made its aid programme more selective. Tunisian 'socialism', it is true, excited the anxieties of many Americans, including some in the labour movement. But as the Kennedy government tried to establish conditions for the giving of aid – essentially that recipient countries should be able to show serious efforts of their own to develop their economy along rational lines – Bourguiba arrived in the United States (in May 1961) able to demonstrate that his government had prepared a plan for economic development which precisely met the American conditions.

The Bizerte incident, which followed so closely on Bourguiba's visit to the United States, did not seriously disturb relations between the two countries; Bourguiba expressed disappointment at the limited support which Tunisia received in the United Nations, but was too experienced a politician to be unaware of the delicacy of the American position between its European ally and Tunisia. The essential fact was that Tunisia continued to fulfil the conditions of an aid/receiving country, and to offer major hopes for the realization of actual success in economic development. It acquired and kept a high priority in the American aid programme – sharing this distinction on the African continent with Nigeria, until the collapse of that country in 1967.

The fresh crisis in Tunisia's relations with France must, therefore, be seen in the context of growing American support and aid – and of small/scale assistance, in 1964, from Kuwait. The break with France was neither total nor final. In May 1966 fresh commercial agreements were signed which gave free entry to a certain number of Tunisian goods, including a small quantity of wine. Above all the Tunisian educational system continued to depend on French assistance. In March 1968 there were three thousand French teachers in Tunisia. One half of the university teachers were French, although the number is diminishing. Tunisian students continued to go to France for higher degrees and young professional men for shorter periods of vocational training. Under French law a certain number of conscripts can undertake overseas service in developing countries instead of military service, and of such young men there were some 900 in Tunisia, many of them as teachers. Civilian employees – teachers and technical experts – are paid more than they would be in France, but one-third of their salary comes from the French government.

The connection with France and the assistance Tunisia receives therefore remains close, is solidly based on widespread French culture in Tunisia and is generally the subject of amicable speeches on both sides of the Mediterranean. On the other hand, the two crises of Bizerte and the nationalization of land meant that Tunisia, having started off with the closest relations with France at the time of the Algerian war and Youssefism, lagged behind Morocco and Algeria in this respect.

With the countries of the Arab Middle East, Tunisian relations rapidly become more strained and more complex. In the spring of 1965 Bourguiba made a journey to the Middle East, at the beginning of which, in Cairo, he seemed to be consolidating the relationship which had built up through 1964 – following the Bizerte celebrations and the Arab summit conferences of that year. He went at a time of diplomatic turmoil. It had transpired at the beginning of the year that the German Federal Republic was planning to supply arms to Israel and, in reply, Nasser had invited Ulbricht to Cairo; his visit followed Bourguiba's by a few days. The German Federal Republic cancelled its plans to sell arms to Israel, but established diplomatic relations with that country, while suspending aid to Egypt; while Nasser stood by his invitation to Ulbricht in spite of German pressure.

Arriving in Cairo, Bourguiba gave support to the Egyptian

position. He spoke publicly of Nasser's leadership of the Arab world and of the threat which deliveries of arms to Israel represented for Palestinians and Arabs. Privately he indicated to Nasser that Tunisia would not break its relations with Bonn, and also indicated that he would not speak publicly about Israel.

But his intentions were swept aside by what he saw in the Middle East. In Jordan he visited refugee camps at Jericho. He was profoundly affected by the way in which the refugees were nourished on 'chimerical hopes and sterile hatred'. Back in Amman he said, 'The Palestinian affair requires a peaceful solution in which there is neither victor nor vanquished.'

Such language was far from acceptable in the atmosphere of the Middle East. Bourguiba was vehemently taken to task in the Arab press, and when he gave a press conference in Beirut was constantly heckled and questioned. His response was typical of his approach to political problems; he spoke of the acceptance of facts and pleaded for a realistic solution 'by stages'. At this time and subsequently he spoke of the existence of Israel as a 'colonial fact'. The term is suitably ambiguous. The implication is that 'colonialism' should be removed but that 'facts' should be accepted – and the appropriate weight could be given to each side of the balance according to time and audience. But the core of the policy remained the same until 1967. Had Bourguiba been the President of a Middle Eastern state, he would have sought negotiation with Israel, aimed at settlement for the refugees and rectification of frontiers in favour of the Arabs. As it was he could do nothing. The Israeli Foreign Minister, Mrs Golda Meir, expressed the readiness of her government to open discussions through Tunisia as an intermediary; but by this time Bourguiba's proposals had evoked such hostility in the Arab countries (his visit to Baghdad having to be cancelled because of demonstrations) that nothing was to be gained along these lines.

The outcome of Bourguiba's visit to the Middle East was, therefore, a renewed conflict between Tunisia and the Arab east. The antagonism was above all between Bourguiba and Nasser. The differences in the government and policies of Tunisia and Egypt were important and profound – as was the difference in personality and background of the two leaders. In themselves, however, they were less important than Nasser's claim to leadership of the Arab world and the readiness of the Egyptian government to intervene in the politics of other Arab states.

In Tunisia itself Nasserism has a certain appeal as it has everywhere in the Arab world. But as long as the pragmatism of the Bourguiba regime brings results the appeal remains limited. Egyptian socialism does not carry much conviction with the activists of the Socialist Destourian party; Nasser's claim to primacy does not seduce those who have an historical awareness of the Tunisian struggle for independence, dating back to the 1930's. Within Tunisia, therefore, support for Nasser and a policy of radical Arabism remains a minority force; but at the same time, the country is bordered by Libya – politically unpredictable, making a bridge between Egypt and the Maghreb – and Algeria, radical although independent of Nasser.

The outcome of the new split with Nasser was that Tunisia alone of the Arab states did not attend the summit conference held in Casablanca in September 1965. Explaining the Tunisian position, Bourguiba claimed that 'no one is secure from Cairo's intrigues' and asserted that in 1963 Nasser had asked for the use of Tunisian airfields to help carry arms to Algeria in support of its frontier dispute with Morocco. Tunisia remained a member of the Arab League but demanded that it should return to its true spirit of respect for the sovereignty of members and co-operation between them.

It was consistent with this policy that Bourguiba should give support to King Faisal of Saudi Arabia in his attempt to counter Nasser's dominance of the Arab world. Faisal's proposal was for a summit conference of Islamic states – including Egypt – which would reinvigorate the Islamic faith in its conflict with materialism and Zionism. The proposal was denounced by Nasser and the radical Arabs as an attempt to establish a reactionary alliance supported by the United States. But when Faisal travelled across the Islamic world (and to the United States) in 1965 and 1966 he was welcomed in Rabat and in Tunis – in spite of the differences between the theocracy of Saudi Arabia and the lay state of Tunisia.

In June 1967 the perspective of the Palestine question changed radically with the eruption of the new six-day war. The result was a strong feeling of solidarity which swept across the Arab world, embracing the Maghreb along with all other Arab states. In the midst of the crisis which preceded the war Bourguiba sent his first message since 1965 to the Secretary-General of the Arab League, and the Tunisian delegation at the U.N. gave up its boycott of meetings of the Arab delegations. With the outbreak of war on 5th June, Bourguiba got into touch directly with Nasser and diplomatic relations were re-established. A military expedition was prepared and despatched towards Egypt – a totally ineffective venture except in showing solidarity with the Arab cause: the army did not get beyond the Libyan frontier before a cease-fire was agreed, and would not easily have been accommodated into the Arab forces if it had.

Meanwhile in Tunis groups of rioters emerged from the medina and marched through the streets burning Jewish, British and American property. The British Embassy was the first to suffer, standing as it does at the gates of the medina; the American Embassy was better defended by marine guards; Jewish shops and the TWA office were burnt; the synagogue was invaded and the rumour spread that there was electronic equipment in it giving contact with Israel. (It turned out to be a gramophone.) Large numbers of Jews packed their bags and left – not to Israel but to France. They followed in the wake of a continuing Jewish emigration since independence – many Jews had kept French citizenship rather than accept Tunisian, and many chose a European rather than an Arab society. A relatively small proportion chose the national state of Israel.

The war did not, however, produce a fundamental change either in the regime or in its foreign policy. The riots of 5 June (which were almost entirely confined to Tunis) were severely condemned by the President and a tax levied on every Tunis household to pay for the damage. Although no settlement has so far emerged from the Arab–Israeli war, Tunisia continued to be one of the most moderate of the Arab states. Bourguiba continued to make speeches which were critical of Nasserism, and to urge students to concentrate on practical tasks of building the country rather than being led astray by ideology. As always he adopted a very moderate tone about the war in Vietnam and stressed the efforts which the United States made towards ending the war.

In the second decade of its independence Tunisia had thus achieved considerable stability in its foreign relations. Its territorial problems were relatively minor – in April 1968 it agreed with Algeria to ask the French National Geographic Institute to make a study of the area in dispute between them, south of Bir Romane, in preparation for a negotiated settlement. Its relations with France had gone through periods of crisis but had never been disrupted, and in the spring of 1968 fresh commercial agreements, as well as provision for the laying of a telephone cable linking Marseilles, Bizerte and Tunis were worked out. The United States was a friendly power and a major supplier of aid, while a parliamentary delegation visited the Soviet Union and technical aid was provided by the countries of eastern Europe.

11   Development and change

BY ANY STANDARDS Tunisia at the moment of independence was
an underdeveloped country. It had a high degree of illiteracy, a pre-
dominantly agricultural economy in which large sectors remained
primitive, a substantial part of the population which did not enter
into the cash economy at all, or, if it did, earned wages of less than
£10 per annum. The legacy from French occupation was significant
but inadequate. The infrastructure of a modern economy had been
established in skeleton form – roads, harbours, public buildings. A
small elite of educated men had been trained in France – though
few of them in practical or technological skills. The exploitation of
the land had led to the development of certain large estates; but it had
disrupted traditional agricultural practice and established little in its
place. French estates were successful at the expense of the surrounding
countryside; they employed relatively little labour and created rural
unemployment around themselves.

Since independence the development of Tunisia has been the
single most overriding purpose of the Tunisian government – which
has not been seriously threatened in its tenure of power, and has
abjured adventurism in foreign affairs. There have been several
distinguishing features of this development, only some of which
have been present in other countries for so long. Political stability is
one of them. Differences of view within the Tunisian government
and administration – between the party and the technicians, between
those who adopt planning for pragmatic reasons and those who are
committed to planning for its own sake – have been, and are,
important; but they have been contained within a single govern-

ment system. The men who led the movement to independence have remained at the head, and they have succeeded in recruiting young men, giving them power and responsibility in a smooth succession.

Not least of the advantages of this stability is that it has permitted pragmatic discussion of the aims and methods of development. It has never been assumed, either, that an increase in the national product and the standard of living is sufficient by itself; or that redistribution should be carried out regardless of the cost in terms of over-all development. No one has supposed that development is possible without fundamental reform of the structure of society; but, whether through initial wisdom or as the result of experience, Tunisian leaders have recognized the strength of tradition, the values it embodies and the limitations it imposes. Finally, they have been quick to see that in politics and economics means become ends, that nothing is more dangerous than to adopt undesirable means to achieve ends, however worthy. Nothing is more permanent than the temporary.

Pragmatism is encouraged by the openness of Tunisia both to technical advice and to research and examination by outsiders. Few developing countries offer better opportunities for research by foreign observers. Stability and continuity of development make possible long-term projects like those conducted by Harvard University in the field of agricultural development, nutrition and health. The Tunisian government has always welcomed such enquiry; it has offered assistance to an unusual degree (for example, in opening bank accounts to facilitate research into agricultural credit) providing interpreters and even financial assistance. Such investigation provides information and resources of factual knowledge which are immensely valuable in themselves; it also reinforces habits of enquiry and pragmatism which in any case are developed in an educational system linked to France.

Open enquiry and sensitivity to the facts of the situation is the more important since the starting-point of development in Tunisia, as elsewhere, is very varied from one part of the country to another. The crowded villages of the Sahel are unlike the Enfida estate, in spite of being so close to it; the Cape Bon is entirely different from the Medjerda valley; the south and centre of the country is different from anywhere on the coast. The differences come not only from climate and soil but from history – from the survival of the Sahel villages even in the time of the Hilalian invasion and from the impact of French colonization in a more recent period.

Tunisian development has benefited not only from the stability of politics but also from the success of the system of government in providing for political mobilization. The task which this involves is not easy nor is its success by any means complete. It consists, in the field of development, of transferring advanced techniques to a traditional environment. The resources of knowledge necessary for development are readily available throughout the world; what is lacking is rather the dissemination of such knowledge – especially in agriculture – and its application. For this the political system of Tunisia makes as much provision as possible, given the shortage of cadres and technicians which still prevails.

Tunisian efforts to develop the economy have evoked and been furthered by aid from more than a dozen foreign countries, as well as from the United Nations and its agencies. The United States is the biggest provider of aid – until the end of 1965 some 40 per cent of the total came from this source. It antedates independence, since Marshall Aid funds were channelled to Tunisia. Since then American aid has been given under all the principal heads of the aid programme. In the early years nearly sixty million dollars were provided in grants providing general economic support – for the importation of products such as sugar, petroleum products, tea, rice, textiles and to finance specific projects. Loans have been made for such projects as the construction of the Nabana River Dam, for Tunis airport and for the establishment of loan funds in agricultural and industrial development banks.

Tunisia has also benefited from the facilities provided by the United States government for the export of food – under the provisions of the famous 'Public Law 480'. Under the provisions of this law wheat is sold to Tunisia at a very small dollar cost; the greater part of the 'payment' is required in Tunisian dinars, which the United States then makes available in the form of loans, or uses

to defray the local costs of projects established under the aid programme. A relatively small proportion is kept by the United States
to cover the cost of some of its own operations in Tunisia. Thus in
the period up to 1967 sales agreements under Title 1 of Public Law
480 were made to a value of nearly 80 million dollars; of this grants
were made to the Tunisian government (in dinars) equivalent to
7 million dollars and another 47 million in grants and long-term
loans for specific projects; the dinar equivalent of nearly $9 million
was made to private persons or companies for the establishment of
businesses in Tunisia and just over $14 millions retained by the
United States for its own needs in Tunisian currency. As the
Tunisian economy grows stronger the terms of such aid become
stiffer. In November 1967 a new agreement required 50 per cent
of the payment to be made in dollars, over a period of 20 years,
instead of the previous ratio of 25/75 dollar to dinar payment.

American wheat has also been provided for Tunisia for use in
welfare and training projects. The World Food Programme,
which was organized under the United Nations as part of its
Freedom from Hunger Campaign (starting in 1962) has made a
major contribution to the same end. The food is used in children's
villages (Villages d'Enfants de Bourguiba) which care for homeless
children. It is also distributed as part of wages, or used in canteens at
training centres. It thereby makes a direct contribution to the cost of
agricultural training, encourages regular attendance and develops
improved dietary habits.

In the period up to 1965 United States aid to Tunisia was four
times that of France – which was interrupted by the crisis of 1964.
The French government gave, above all, cultural and technical
assistance, financing teachers and technical advisers. The French
government has also made loans, of which the most recent provides
for the submarine cable linking Tunisia to France. The German
Federal Republic has been a major source of aid, especially in the
form of technical assistance. It has projects which furnish training
for hotel work, and in mechanical skills, and has also supplied
technical assistance in agriculture and cattle breeding. In addition to
technical assistance the German government has recently contributed

loans for the development of ports at Mahdia and Tabarka, airports at Monastir and Jerba, roads and high-tension cables. Like the United States, Germany also has volunteers working in Tunisia, giving informal training in such skills as sewing and carpentry.

The list of technical assistance and other aid offered to Tunisia is a long one. Swedes give assistance in the development of fishing at Kelibia; the Soviet Union has provided credits on a large scale – comparable to France – although only a small proportion has been taken up; Kuwait, Czechoslovakia, Yugoslavia and Poland as well as Denmark and Holland have supplied assistance and/or credit.

Aid of this sort has been arranged by bilateral agreement. In addition, the United Nations has made a major contribution through its specialized agencies. The Food and Agriculture Organization has carried out research (financed by the UN Special Fund) into agricultural methods and techniques suitable for the development of the dry central region of Tunisia. Two centres, Ouled M'hammed and Ousseltia, were chosen for this purpose – sited in very different areas (having only aridity in common) – to explore methods of water and soil conservation and mixed farming. Reforestation has been undertaken by FAO. At the same time UNESCO, with money from the Special Fund and the Tunisian government, has carried out research into the use of brackish water for irrigation. These are only some of the examples of research and practical development which the UN has provided.

The stability and continuity of Tunisian government gives an incentive for outside aid. It also offers a necessary condition for the use of such aid, the co-ordination of a wide range of technical assistance and the drawing of benefit from it. The central direction and planning of economic development began in 1961. From independence until then, state interference in economic life was minimal; but the withdrawal of French capital and trained personnel led to the stagnation of the economy to the point where government intervention was imperative. A Ministry of Planning was established with Ahmed ben Salah at its head; the Ministry drew up a 'ten year perspective' together with a 'three year plan' (from 1962 to 1965) which was followed by a 'four year plan' up to 1968.

This institutional development is important in relation to outside aid. It provides a solid core of Tunisian direction such that the Tunisian government can to the best of its ability choose the direction of the economy and the scope and scale of development. The United States government, at least in the mid-sixties, maintained a USAID office in Tunis with a staff of nearly one hundred; the UN kept a permanent mission under the direction of a resident representative (Dr Mir Khan) and it was imperative, therefore, that the Tunisian government should not be overbalanced by this considerable foreign establishment.

The plans themselves are set in the context of Destourian Socialism. The aim of development, in the words of the first plan, is not development for its own sake but for the benefit of all social classes in proportion to their efforts and also their needs. The second plan continues the same theme: the prime objective is man, and Destourian Socialism does not load itself with the concerns of foreign ideologies like a violent class struggle or the *étatisation* of the economy.

The plans have set four broad objectives of economic and social development: decolonization – completed by the end of the first plan – reform of economic structures including industrialization of the country, human development – including education, formation of cadres, the fight against illiteracy and unemployment – and self-development, so that investment can come from internal resources rather than being excessively dependent on foreign assistance.

The effectiveness and the importance to Tunisia of planned development can be judged in a number of different ways. The sheer volume of input and the reform of structures is undoubtedly impressive, and so is the output that has followed. Bilateral aid in the period up to 1965 amounted to approximately £60 million actually delivered. According to United States estimates output increased between 1961 and 1965 by 20 per cent, investment increased by 42 per cent to reach an annual proportion of 25 per cent of the gross domestic product. Growth rate in this period was of the order of 6–7 per cent, although a bad harvest in 1966 lowered it to 2 per cent.

New industries have been developed; among the most important of them has been tourism, which has required large-scale investment in hotel buildings and a massive effort in the training of hotel workers. Existing industries have been expanded under government direction and with government and foreign finance. The textile industry was brought under a National Textile Office in 1962 and three companies established – in cotton, wool and clothing – which have expanded existing capacity (especially at Ksar-Hellal) and added new factories. Industries which were monopolized by France before independence have been developed by the Tunisian government – the banks have been nationalized; the merchant marine built up so that part of the country's trade is carried in Tunisian ships. The fishing industry has been developed under the dynamic leadership of Mahmoud El Ghoul, Director of the National Fishing Office. The industry has acquired new vessels and fishermen have been trained in the use of them. The distributive side of the industry has been developed so that fish is delivered to shops belonging to the National Office in inland towns and the fishermen are not obliged to sell their catch as quickly as possible on the quayside (although the private sale of fish continues). Above all, immense progress has been made in the development and rational use of water resources.

Progress of this over-all sort must be set against the immensity of the problem which confronts a country with scant resources. In wheat production Tunisia's problems have increased rather than diminished: the natural deterioration of the land and the withdrawal of the French meant that wheat production fell by 30 per cent in the fifteen years up to 1968 while the consumption of wheat increased as a result of population growth and increased standards of living. In 1966 (a bad year) imports cost over $13 million – though the cost was largely borne by the US government and the UN. At the end of 1967 fifty tons of seed of a new strain of wheat, developed in Mexico, were brought to Tunisia as a result of a co-operative effort between the government, USAID and the Rockefeller Foundation in the hope of contributing substantially to the problem of wheat growing.

The population of Tunisia increases, according to Tunisian estimates, by 2.2 per cent per annum; independent estimates suggest a figure of 2.8 per cent. The Ford Foundation financed and helped establish a programme of family planning in 1965; initially the objective was to fit a contraceptive device for women who already had four children. But in the summer of 1966 Bourguiba made a speech which indicated his caution with regard to family planning, either because it met with resistance amongst the people or because he feared it would limit the growth of the elite while allowing the more backward population to increase unchecked. In any case family planning has yet to outweigh the effect of improved hygiene and health on population growth.

An expanding population means that a high proportion are young. It imposes an immense burden on the programme of school-building and the fight against illiteracy; the more so since research shows that 'crash programmes' are of limited effectiveness and that a minimum number of years are indispensable if reading and writing skills are to be retained rather than dissipated in a very short space of time.

Even industrial development does not always bring the success expected of it. USAID provided some $7 million for the construction and equipment of a factory at Kasserine to produce high-quality paper from esparto grass, which grows freely in the surrounding region. It was an ambitious project, but it appears to have installed the wrong machines for the grass, and USAID reported that 'due to technical difficulties as yet unresolved' the plant had not reached capacity. 'Once these difficulties are eliminated the plant could provide Tunisia with foreign exchange earning up to $5 m. a year.'[1]

Whatever figures are chosen, the result of an examination of aggregate progress in Tunisian development are impressive and daunting at the same time. Vegetable production increased from 260,000 tons in 1958 to 400,000 tons in 1964; 60 million plants a year were distributed to market gardeners; 12 million fruit trees were established in ten government nurseries. At the same time work camps were still necessary (in the spring of 1968) because not all Tunisian men could be usefully employed within the economic system; German assistance provided for the training of 200 students at Menzel-Bourguiba in mechanical skills, but only a quarter of those who graduated in 1967 found employment. Agricultural wages were increased by 26 per cent in the spring of 1968 – to a dollar a day for eight hours' work. Much of the effort in farming reform will take years to bring a return, since it consists in the trans‑formation of wheat‑ and wine‑growing areas to fruit‑growing. Pistachios take twenty years to reach full crop.

In many respects Tunisia faces problems similar to those of other developing countries. The United Nations Conference on Trade and Development, which met in New Delhi at the beginning of 1968, was concerned with the plight of the developing countries in a world where *per capita* income increased thirty times faster in developed countries than underdeveloped; raw materials prices fell by 7 per cent over ten years while the price of industrial products increased by 10 per cent. But although the problems are common to the developing world, Tunisia can claim that it maintains a continuous effort devoted to their solution, following rational principles and with pragmatic planning as far as this is possible, in conditions of political stability and with the benefit of large‑scale foreign aid.

Progress can be judged in aggregate terms; it can also be examined in the experience of particular projects. Thus Ousseltia – forty miles west of Kairouan on the arid plateau of central Tunisia – has achieved a reputation for its livestock production. Its achievement is to establish a system of mixed farming which integrates grass and crop growth with animal husbandry. It is only possible as a result of a system of terraces and drainage which combat the storms of late summer and make the most of the rain which falls in that brief period.

At Ouled M'Hammed, the other FAO centre in central Tunisia, a different small economy has been established, surrounding a deep well which brings water up from some 1,500 feet. Irrigation from the well makes possible the cultivation of apricots, lemons, almonds, oranges, peaches and pears. These are spectacular projects whose success is obvious to the eye – trees and grass grow where there was none before, and livestock are raised. In economic terms the building of small dams to irrigate the citrus orchards of the Cape Bon, the

194

development of agricultural credit available to small farmers, may be more advantageous – and it is indeed in this area that agricultural output has shown the most marked growth. But the problem is social and national as well as economic – a question of diminishing the gulf between the prosperity of the coast and the interior.

In the Medjerda valley, farming by French settlers showed a major improvement on traditional methods of cultivation. But before independence, it in turn had proved inefficient, both in terms of its deprivation of the soil, and in comparison with farming elsewhere. At the end of French rule government intervention, with the assistance of Marshall aid, brought the beginnings of an improvement scheme and the building of dams. After independence the Tunisian government established the *Office de la Mise en Valeur de la Medjerda* and took over the development of the valley, with a plan for irrigation, erosion control, land reform and light manufacturing. By the beginning of 1967 three out of five dams had been completed and an area of 62,000 acres (out of 176,000 planned for 1971) had been irrigated. Plans which the French government had made for erosion control have been implemented, and a quarter of the hill country afforested and terraced. A landreform measure was passed at the same time as the institution of the Office, and it was supplemented by the agreement with France for the takeover of French lands in 1963, then by the nationalization law of 1964. Land which thus came to the Office was then sold to Tunisians, with twentyyear credit. To be eligible as a purchaser a Tunisian had to meet certain important conditions – above all to have some capability in irrigation farming, to be able to read and write, to be between twenty and thirty years old and not have more than three children, and to have sufficient capital to make a start with his plot. In addition he had to be without land before his purchase.

Every attempt has thus been made to prevent the area slipping back to inefficient exploitation. Land is farmed in state farms until it is sold; individual farmers are selected according to their promise as efficient farmers, and they then raise the crops the Office requires by methods it advocates; farmers belong to credit and service cooperatives which provide equipment and marketing beyond the scale of individual farmers. The whole project has been supported by foreign aid – including US aid to the extent of more than $200,000.

The success of the Medjerda project has made one of its main centres, the village of El Habibia, a showpiece of modern Tunisia. Land which used to be covered with flood water in winter and parched dry in summer has been brought into use; the sharp contrast between wealthy, efficient foreign estates and a poor backward indigenous agriculture has been broken down. Day workers in the valley used to earn six shillings a day; now about half the private farmers earn £200 a year, a quarter of them less and another quarter more, up to £400.

But the Medjerda valley is not the whole of Tunisia; it represents some 4 per cent of the *arable* land and will provide for 5 per cent of the farming population. Capital investment in this relatively small sector of the economy is very high, and some of it appears unjustified in view of the relatively small number of people – and the small amount of agricultural activity – which it supports. In the long run the success of the project must be judged, not solely within the Medjerda valley, but in its exemplary effect in Tunisia as a whole.

The Tunisian achievement and prospects can thus be judged by surveying the economy as a whole, or by examining specific projects like Ousseltia or the Medjerda valley. But in another area innovation was met by mounting resistance. This was in the establishment of co-operatives, intended to be the specifically Tunisian contribution to the problem of development in agriculture and in commerce. In 1962 Bourguiba characterized part of this problem when he spoke of the need to 'reconcile two contradictory imperatives' – the stimulus of private ownership and the tools and techniques which at present are unknown to the small farmer. The Tunisian government was never tempted by state collectivization following the communist pattern; yet it did not wish to forego the advantages of large-scale enterprises in agriculture of the sort the French had developed, or of a kind which the future made possible. Moreover the French estates were productive because of technical knowledge

provided by agricultural experts in private employment; in independent Tunisia these could only be replaced slowly, by government
training and payment, and must be used to the maximum advantage
– as they could not be in a system of peasant ownership.[2]

Agricultural co-operatives began before the first plan. As the
Tunisian government acquired the farms of settlers – by agreement
with the French government – it established production co-
operatives by grouping Tunisian properties surrounding a French
estate into a single unit. Elsewhere similar groups were constructed
without the nucleus of a settler estate. Landowners maintained their
title to their land, but they surrendered control of management to an
administrative council of the co-operative.

The institution of co-operatives initiated a process which has
gathered strength up to the present time. The land available increased with the nationalization of the French estates in 1964, but
this fact was less important than the pressures which were created on
the economy by the retaliatory measures of the French government,
and the consequent urgent need for successful mobilization of the
agricultural sector. In 1968 the principle of co-operation was
extended from the agricultural sphere to that of retail trading, and
the small-scale Jerbian grocers who formed so characteristic a part
of the Tunisian towns were grouped into co-operatives by the
Tunisian process of reasoned compulsion.

At the same time a change of emphasis had come about in the
ethos of the programme of co-operatives. Initially they were seen as a
means of bringing technological innovation. From the time of the
second plan they were increasingly political as well as technological.[3]
The ideological and political importance of the co-operative form
of organization is set out in the statement of the objectives of the
quadrennial plan in these words:

> The Co-operative, to the extent that it is authentic, and the
> Tunisian state works to make it so, is a unity of production
> organized according to the democratic principle, bringing about
> the placing in common of the means of production or of certain
> services and functioning at once in its interest as a micro-collectivity

and in the general interest . . . at once a unity of production and a school, [the Co-operative] fits perfectly our ideological pre-occupations.[4]

The plan was right to see the co-operative as a school, since its successful establishment calls for a major transformation of the values and habits of society – whether it be the beduin society of the south, the village of the Sahel or that of the north. There were in fact complex human and political obstacles to overcome in the successful establishment of co-operatives. The first was to provide cadres, technical and managerial, who would introduce modern methods of agriculture – crop diversification, the use of machines, methodical cultivation – and carry the momentum on which the plan depends down into the villages and the land. The second was to institutionalize and internalize the values and habits of work on which the co-operative depends amongst the people responsible for its functioning.

In the first task the Tunisian government did achieve some success, given the scope and the nature of the task involved – not least the very magnitude of training enough men for the job. The second was a far more fundamental task. It meant introducing concepts of democracy and participation which are new to Tunisian – and Arab – society. It involved changing attitudes to the land, replacing the deep supposition that land belongs to the man who tills it with the more sophisticated notion of sharing implicit in a co-operative. It required the acceptance of social relationships which cut across family and kinship ties. And it follows from all this that the task of the cadres was not simply to transfer agricultural techniques, but to act as the agents of a profound social change, to establish a relationship between an essentially middle-class political movement, deeply influenced by western values and training, and a traditional peasant, beduin and village society.

The difficulties which such a change involves have been shown in the history of the co-operatives. Given the reforming rather than revolutionary nature of Tunisian development, it was inevitable that the first steps should be taken through the intermediary of the established authorities. The result was that the local sheikhs summoned the peasants in order to draw up the boundaries of the co-operatives and, rather than explaining what was to be done, said that it was part of a 'government plan'. Similarly the election of the first officials of the co-operatives drew on established authorities – of three administrators, for example, there would be two drawn from the notable families.

The very construction of co-operative villages demonstrated difficulties in moulding new habits out of old traditions. An attempt was made in the north to adapt the technical plan of a co-operative village to the traditional arrangements, including the distribution of households according to their family and background. Even so the peasants were reluctant to live in houses which may be too cold in winter and too hot in summer and, more important, do not make provision for elderly relatives, or for the cow – which for the peasant of the north is an element of security as is the olive tree for the Sahelian or Sfaxian.[5] The establishment of the co-operatives was pushed ahead with speed against growing resistance. In January 1968 Ahmed Mestiri resigned in protest from the government. In the spring of 1969 the police and army were involved in violent clashes with the villagers of the Sahel. Finally, in September 1969, the development of the co-operatives was arrested and Ahmed ben Salah, its main architect, removed from the Ministry of National Economy and, later, from the Education Ministry.

The problems of change can be seen in an especially acute form in the island of Jerba. The history of the island has been one of constant invasion and attack, in spite of which its special character has survived intact, so that it makes a direct link with the earliest days of Tunisia's history. The amphors which the potters make are still those of classical Greece; the fronts of the spinners' workshops have the form of a Greek temple – a functionally useless façade to a vaulted building. The physical characteristics of a Mediterranean people have survived; so has the Berber language and the rigorous discipline of the Kharijite religion.

Over a thousand years and more a rhythm of life established itself on the island. On the land the rhythm is determined by the seasons and the annual cycle of date-palms and olive trees. Nearly two-thirds of the agricultural product of the island comes from these two sources. Vines are also grown, so are fig trees; in a small area around Mahboubine and Cedghiane sweet water permits the growth of apples, almonds, citrus and pomegranates. Work on the fruit trees is interspersed with sowing and reaping; when agricultural work ceases in the summer, attention is turned instead to handicrafts.

Jerba produces above all woollen bed covers and pots. The whole process of the making of covers is based on a subtle and intimate structure of economic and social relationships. Wool is imported into Jerba from the mainland and from abroad – the warp comes mainly from England and France, the weft from Tunisia (a small proportion is grown on Jerba). The importation is in the hands of a dozen merchants, who then distribute it to a large number of women who wash it and others who spin. Traditionally washers and spinners retain two-thirds of the spun wool in payment – a system which worked well in spite of the fact that there is a fifty to sixty per cent variation in the loss of weight in the course of washing, combing and spinning. For the most part, monetary payment has now replaced the old arrangements; but the honesty which characterizes the distribution of work and profit between a few merchants and a large number of widely dispersed workers is outstanding. As Salah-Eddine Tlatli has written:

> Here intervenes a fundamental element of the whole Jerba economy: a scrupulous honesty. The agricultural worker often works by himself, as does the fisherman, the spinner or the merchant. No control is possible. And yet in this circle of association on which the whole economic system rests there is never any fraud but confidence and general honesty. These same qualities have been the foundation of all the commercial and industrial Jerbian enterprises on the mainland.[6]

The spinners achieve an extraordinary fineness of weave, using light spindles made from olive wood, sometimes passing the thread through a hole in their fingernail to make it finer, producing some 3,500 metres of thread in a kilogram. Then the wool goes to an industrial dyeworks where standards of colour are maintained before being distributed again to weavers – some, scattered over a large part of the island, having a single loom, others with workshops in the towns. The final product is one of the finest coming from Tunisia in the quality of craftsmanship, durability, colour and price.

The craft of pottery, which is concentrated at Guelala, is even more ancient than weaving – since weaving began with the decline of the Phoenician and Roman craft of dyeing. The preparation of the clay, the methods used to shape the pots, the rooms in which the work is done, the kilns – all are unchanged at least since classical times.

But the ancient lineage of agriculture and industry in Jerba does not now ensure its survival; nor does it accord with modern notions of social justice. Since the war there has been an immense migration of Jerbians from the island. The emigration was provoked in part by the decline of agriculture, attributable to the division and sub-division of the land into small plots. In 1950 approximately 100,000 acres were divided between 45,000 farmers. Emigration of able-bodied men further destroys the prosperity of agriculture – although the emigrants send home remittances on an impressive scale. (In 1961 nearly half a million pounds was received in the Jerbian post offices, when the population of the island was between 60,000 and 65,000.)

Agriculture is inefficient and holdings are too small; they are divided up into small parcels, so that a farmer may own part of a tree here and part somewhere else. Olive trees are frequently in need of replacement and more rational planting; irrigation is by a system of wells from which camels draw water.

For such a society, what can development mean? It has already meant the intrusion of one of the most modern sectors of the Tunisian economy – the tourism industry. Hotels have been built and an airport makes possible the influx of tourists from Europe, two or three hours away. Coming in search of the sun and unable to bring motor cars with them, the tourists so far penetrate little into the island; they remain an isolated unit in a land where the Phoenicians still seem close at hand. The hotels create a demand for market-gardening products which the island could well meet; it can only do so after a reform of agricultural practice, which is called for in any case since old techniques have worn themselves out. Yet what must change is an intimately integrated and finely balanced society which is almost a biological unit.

Tunisian leaders have shown their sensitivity to problems of this order. Continuous efforts are made to maintain traditional crafts intact and to make them viable economically. This is the task of the National Office of Artisanat, which was established with branches in all major towns. It provides facilities in which traditional crafts can be practised. One of these is the carpet workshop in Kairouan, in a building originally constructed by the French as a display centre. There, women can take up casual work. They do not need to borrow money to buy an ancient loom to clutter up their own home, if they choose to earn hourly wages in the workshop. In other towns teenage girls are set to work making rugs and covers in traditional regional designs. The Artisanat also provides outlets for artisan products – both in attractive showrooms like that on the Avenue Habib Bourguiba in Tunis, and abroad.

Yet vigorous as such crafts may be they have never in the past provided an adequate standard of living for Tunisians, even when the population was smaller than it is now. Admirable as the values of traditional society may be they have not in the past guaranteed peace and security; nor are they so highly regarded that educated men and women wish to preserve them unchanged.

Sometimes change comes easily. Let us imagine a house on the edge of Sfax. It stands in a large garden – a garden which is not close-packed with flowers and vegetables as it might be in England but in which trees are carefully spaced to take advantage of the dew, which is their main source of water. Amongst them are two pomegranate trees – 'Granada apples' as the French named them. The fruit appears as a symbol of fertility itself – and is, for in some parts of the country ploughing starts with the crushing of a pomegranate over the ploughshare.

The house is square. It appears bare to the outside, because it is built round an internal courtyard. Rooms open off on all sides, shaded and cool, sheltered from the harsh winds of both winter and summer. In one of these rooms men visitors may be received. The owner of the house is a moderately well-to-do trader in olive oil who, with some skill and much patience, has constructed a lute which his son plays, while his brother performs on the accordion. Somewhere in the background the women of the house flit past, catching a quick curious look at the visitors, but not appearing before them.

The house was made to be secure. It was built when the memory of tribes coming in from the desert, in a year of drought, was still fresh. Its courtyard construction gives it protection; the garden is surrounded by a high mud wall surmounted in places with prickly pear. Against one of the outside walls is the *basse cour* – a smaller courtyard where the animals and poultry reside. It is secure, too, in having a store of food – beans, dried vegetables, herbs and spices of every kind, dry and kept in large stone jars, as they always have been, together with olive oil.

From the roof of the house one looks across the circle of gardens that surround Sfax, to the long lines of olives beyond. The roof is flat, and on it are the bases for new walls. The owner's father intended that his son should be able to construct an additional floor to provide living space for a further generation, or for more sons. But this has not happened. His daughter has married a manager, and they have set up house a short distance away. It is built like a French house, with a verandah at the front. Here the newly married woman of the house answers the door and admits the guests. She is young and attractive, dressed in a cotton frock, but she, like her brothers, speaks French. She is eager to show the house to her guests, even though it involves some complicated manoeuvring; for her husband's mother is there, with an aunt and a friend, and they have no wish to meet male strangers face to face. So when the guests wish to move from the kitchen into the living-room they must first move into the bed-room, and somehow contrive to move from there back to the kitchen to allow the guests to take their place – while all the time curiosity fights with modesty for control of their movements.

The house is elegantly furnished in what might be called Belgian style – sideboard, bed, wardrobe in veneered wood with a surface of extreme shine and smoothness – testimony to the accrued wealth of trading in olive oil. It is shown, as well it may be, with glowing pleasure of ownership. The kitchen is endowed with comparable riches. Water comes from a cistern, but can be lifted up, cool and fresh, in a bucket from inside the kitchen itself. There is a calor gas stove for the cooking and an enamelled sink.

The change goes deep. The square house round a courtyard is a pattern established over centuries across the Arab world. Such houses, especially when they were poorer than the one at Sfax, never provided an easy means to get rid of the refuse and waste of men and animals; the enclosure of the courtyard preserved with equal impartiality the still air of a clean house and of one that accumulated muck. New houses follow a newer, more European pattern. At a more basic level they have to be built with the utmost simplicity. Where the government has worked to stabilize a semi-nomad population it has installed families in the very simplest form of concrete shelter, to ease the transition from a *gourbi* constructed of mud, branches, and anything that came to hand.

But change can only be brought about with the risk of promoting instability and resentment. Those who plan the development of Tunisia can see with ease the advantage to be gained from planting almond trees rather than olives, or from modernizing agriculture. But the individual peasant knows nothing of the balance of payments; for him the change is in a way of life, and even a system of values. A young party secretary can do his best to promote the objectives of the plan; but he must win acceptance from villagers accustomed to a more traditional structure of authority – for whom, even, the more static authority of the French may by now have acquired a rosy hue with the passage of time.

Bourguiba's concept of change in Tunisia relies on the training of cadres who, in turn, will act as leaders throughout society. But young men and women who are educated at the university do not necessarily accept either Bourguiba's ethos or the role he would have them play in the state. They may become intellectuals concerned to be critical and to create an ideology of their own, and there is always the danger that Bourguiba's government will over-react in repressive measures against such exploration and experimentation of ideas.

In common with other developing countries, Tunisia treads a narrow path, unable and unwilling to remain a static and impoverished society, yet courting the dangers of instability and upheaval as it seeks to progress.

It is beset with hazards. In the autumn of 1969 the establishment of co-operatives was arrested. Across the eastern frontier, in Libya, a brisk revolution ended the rule of King Idris and established a government of young officers and civilians professing the ideology of Arab socialism. On both sides Tunisia faced oil-rich neighbours taking a 'progressive' stance and committed to Arab radicalism (whatever the actual conservatism of Algeria's domestic policy).

To these political difficulties was added a natural disaster of the first magnitude. As Bourguiba struggled to recover from hepatitis his country was covered by floods of unsurpassed destructiveness. Not only the mountainous area near the Algerian frontier but the whole country was deluged with storms and rainfall. Neither the natural terrain nor man-made constructions could rapidly disperse the floods which stretched from three miles south of Tunis to Gafsa, inundated Béja and Nabeul, isolated Kairouan. River beds which normally carried a trickle of water and occasionally canalized a flash flood now became torrents hundreds of yards wide. They deposited a sediment many feet deep on the surrounding land, suffocating plants and livestock alike. Help from Morocco and France, relief from international organizations brought some respite. But the destruction wrought on twelve years' agricultural development was immense.

Is political development equally vulnerable to natural disaster? In any historical record the achievements of Bourguiba, from nationalist opposition to government stability, are secure. But the longer personal leadership survives the greater is the problem of succession. Tunisia can no more escape this central crisis of politics than it can command the weather. Its resilience in the face of these hazards will be of importance to the world; and decisive for its own future.

Notes on the Text

1 NATION AND LAND

1 Arabic for 'West'. The Maghreb includes Morocco, Algeria and Tunisia, and sometimes Libya; the east (i.e. the Middle East) is the Mashrek.
2 See André Chouraqui, *Les Juifs d'Afrique du Nord* (Paris, 1952).

2 CARTHAGE

1 Nevill Barbour, *A Survey of North West Africa* (London, 1959), pp. 7–8.
2 Massinissa did his best to survive and profit from the conflict between Rome and Carthage, but his grandson Jugurtha died in captivity in Rome; in the twentieth century they were still heroes in Berber opposition to the French (Barbour, *op. cit.,* pp. 9–10).
3 St Augustine was told that the country folk of Roman Africa called themselves *Chenani*. He thought – possibly because he wanted to class them among the Chosen People – that this was a mispronunciation for *Cananei*. See P. Brown, 'Christianity and Local Culture in Late Roman Africa', *Journal of Roman Studies* (1968).
4 Diodorus, XX, 8, 2–4; cited by Sabatino Moscati, *The Phoenicians* (London, 1968), pp. 126–7.
5 See Moscati, *op. cit.,* pp. 182–3.
6 See G. Charles-Picard, *La Civilisation de l'Afrique Romaine* (Paris, 1959), p. 193.
7 Michael Grant, *The World of Rome* (London, 1960), p. 81.
8 My debt in what follows to the outstanding biography by Peter Brown, *Augustine of Hippo* (London, 1967), is obvious.
9 Brown, *op. cit.,* p. 324.
10 This passage is quoted by Joseph Vogt in *The Decline of Rome* (transl. Janet Sondheimer, London, 1967) pp. 228–9.

3 MUSLIM RULE AND HILALIAN INVASION

1 Bernard Lewis, *The Arabs in History* (London, 1958), p. 55.
2 The Shi'ite dynasty was named after Muhammad's daughter Fatima.
3 G. Marçais, *Les Arabes en Berberie* (Paris, 1913), p. 32.
4 Ibn Khaldun, *The Muqaddimah* (transl. Franz Rosenthal, New York, 1958), Vol. 1, p. 303.

4 THE HAFSIDS AND IBN KHALDUN

1 Quoted by Rosenthal in his introduction to *The Muqaddimah*, p. iii.
2 The record of this meeting has survived; see the translation and commentary by W. J. Fischel, *Ibn Khaldun and Tamerlane* (Berkeley, 1952).
3 *The Muqaddimah*, I, pp. 55–6.
4 *Ibid.*, I, p. 78.
5 *Ibid.*, I, p. 71.
6 *Ibid.*, II, p. 291.
7 Quoted by Robert Brunschvig, *La Berberie orientale sous les Hafsides* (2 vols., Paris, 1940, 1947), p. 238.
8 See Salah-Eddine Tlatli, *Djerba, l'île des Lotophages* (Tunis, 1967).

5 OTTOMAN RULE: TUNISIA OF THE BEYS

1 The legends surrounding the Barbarossas are innumerable: I have relied on the account given by Sir Godfrey Fisher in *Barbary Legend* (Oxford, 1957).
2 It is usually said that Khair-al-Din made himself a vassal of the Ottoman Sultan in order to have military assistance from Constantinople: but see Fisher for a more careful examination of his relationship with the Ottomans.
3 F. Braudel, *La Méditerranée et le monde méditerranéen à l'époque de Philippe II* (Paris, 1966), Vol. II, p. 285.
4 *Ibid.*, II, p. 184.
5 *Ibid.*, II, pp. 191–2.
6 E. Blaquière, *Letters from the Mediterranean* (London, 1813), Vol. II, pp. 200–1.
7 I follow the account given by Fisher, *op. cit.*, pp. 217–27.
8 Blake's letters, cited by Fisher, p. 219.
9 Cited by Fisher, p. 159.
10 *Description de l'Afrique, traduite du Flamand d'O. Dapper* (Amsterdam, 1686), p. 190.
11 The President's palace and the French Embassy are there now.
12 Blaquière, *op. cit.*, Vol. II, pp. 216–17.

13 His account is edited by J. H. Moore in *A New and Complete Collection of Voyages and Travels* (London, 1785?), Vol. II.

14 G. A. Jackson, *Algiers, being a complete Picture of the Barbary States* (London, 1817), pp. 51–2.

15 *Ibid.*, pp. 250–1.

16 *Ibid.*, p. 61.

17 Blaquière, *op. cit.*, Vol. II, pp. 163–4.

6 FRENCH OCCUPATION

1 Jean Ganiage, *Les Origines du protectorat français en Tunisie* (Paris, 1959), pp. 90–3.

2 For an account of Khair-al-Din's work, see A. Hourani, *Arabic Thought in the Liberal Age, 1798–1939* (London, 1962), pp. 84–95.

3 Ganiage, *op. cit.*, pp. 26–7.

4 Letter of 15 October 1880. Archives Nationales, F 19. 2487.

5 Archives du Ministère des Affaires étrangères, *Mémoires et Documents*, Tunisie 11, 1881–2, dated February 1882. See also J. J. Jusserand, *What Me Befell* (London, 1933), Ch. V.

6 *Mémoires et Documents*, Tunisie 14.

7 TUNISIAN NATIONALISM

1 Jacques Berque, *French North Africa* (London, 1967), p. 35.

2 Out of 774,677 of school age, 63,240 in French or Franco-Arab schools, 19,435 in modern Koranic schools, 40,000 in *kouttabs*. Paul Sebag, *Tunisie* (Paris, 1961), p. 181.

3 Leon Carl Brown, *Tunisia Under the French Protectorate* (unpublished thesis, Harvard University, 1962), pp. 52–3.

4 Berque, *op. cit.*, p. 81.

5 *La Tunisie Martyre* (Paris, 1920), pp. 45–6.

6 Bourguiba, *La Tunisie et la France* (Paris, 1954), p. 179.

7 *Ibid.*, p. 186.

8 See Lukasz Hirszowicz, *The Third Reich and The Arab East* (London, 1966), Ch. XIV.

9 Willard A. Beling, *Modernization and African Labor. A Tunisian Case-Study* (New York, 1965), pp. 50–1.

10 Dwight Ling, *Tunisia* (Bloomington, 1967), p. 139.

11 Bourguiba, *op. cit.*, p. 448.

1 23 February 1931. Bourguiba, *Articles de Presse 1929–34* (Tunis, 1967), p. 25.
2 C. Geertz, *Religion in Java* (London, 1960), p. 121.
3 In 1969, at the age of eighty-five, he was decorated by Bourguiba with the Grand Cordon of Independence.

1 Taking its name from the mosque, in turn named after the olive tree beside which it once stood.
2 See Clement Moore, *Tunisia Since Independence* (London, 1965), p. 59.
3 *Ibid.*, p. 85 *n.*
4 See Lars Rudebeck, *Party and People* (Stockholm, 1967), p. 248 *n.*
5 Moore, *op. cit.*, p. 74.
6 The size of each committee is determined in rough proportion to the number of party members in the region. Rudebeck, *op. cit.*, pp. 114 *ff.*
7 I generalize from the study made by Nadia Abu Zahra in an unpublished thesis of the University of Oxford. In the village of Sidi Ameur, near Sousse, party membership increased from 80 to 190.

1 Figures compiled by *La Documentation française* from U.N. statistics. *Maghreb*, Vol. 26, p. 35.

1 *A Report of Ten Years of Operations of the U.S. Assistance Program in Tunisia* (USAID, Washington, D.C., 1967).
2 In 1966, ten years after independence, the number of agricultural technicians was only a third that of the colonial period. See Abdel Kader Zghal, 'Systèmes politiques et structures agraires', *Revue Tunisienne des sciences sociales* (Jan. 1968).
3 In what follows I have drawn on the article by Zghal, 'Système de parenté et système co-operatif', *Rev. Tun. sci. soc.* (Oct. 1967).
4 *Plan Quadriennal 1965–68* (Sécrétariat d'Etat au Plan et a l'économie national Tunis, n.d.), p. 13.
5 Zghal, *loc. cit.*, p. 105.
6 Tlatli, *Djerba*, p. 130.

Acknowledgments

Photographs taken by the author, 4, 6–9, 13, 17, 20, 21; Musée du Bardo, Tunisia, 1, 5; by courtesy of the Trustees of the British Museum, 2, 14, engraving by Agostino Veneziano, 12; J. Allan Cash, 18, 26; Tunisian Embassy, London, 15, 16, 23–25, 27; Tunisian Trade Office, 19; Roger Wood, 3, 10, 11, 22.

Select Bibliography

There are few general works on Tunisia in English; an excellent survey of the whole of the Maghreb up to the end of French rule is however provided by Nevill Barbour, *A Survey of North West Africa* (London, 1959). Geographical description is provided in the indispensable works of Jean Despois: J. Despois and R. Raynal, *Géographie de l'Afrique du Nord-Ouest* (Paris, 1967), J. Despois, *La Tunisie, ses régions* (Paris, 1961), and J. Despois, *La Tunisie orientale, Sahel et Basse-steppe* (Paris, 1955). Valuable too is the volume produced by the Naval Intelligence Division during the second world war entitled *Tunisia*.

The best general historical account is to be found in Charles-André Julien, *Histoire de l'Afrique du Nord*, 2 vols. (Paris, 1951–2), which goes to 1830, and *L'Afrique du Nord en Marche* (Paris, 1952), covering the period before independence.

A short account of the Phoenicians is provided in Donald Harden, *The Phoenicians* (London, 1963) which has an extensive bibliography; and in the longer Sabatino Moscati, *The Phoenicians* (London, 1968). For Roman Africa Mommsen's *Provinces* is still worth reading but for a more up-to-date survey see Gilbert Charles-Picard, *La Civilisation de l'Afrique romaine* (Paris, 1959) and A. H. M. Jones, *The Later Roman Empire* (Oxford, 1964). Peter Brown's *Augustine of Hippo* (London, 1967) is not only a brilliantly perceptive study but includes a comprehensive bibliography. For those who have a taste for monumental works there is Stéphane Gsell, *Histoire ancienne de l'Afrique du Nord*, 8 vols. (Paris, 1913–28).

The period from the Arab conquest to the Ottoman period has been studied in detail by Georges Marçais in *Les Arabes en Berberie* (Paris, 1913) and *La Berberie musulmane et l'Orient au Moyen-âge* (Paris, 1946): and in Robert Brunschvig, *La Berberie Orientale sous les Hafsides* (Paris, 1940). The authoritative work on Islamic art is G. Marçais, *Manuel d'art musulman*, 2 vols. (Paris, 1926–7). For Ibn Khaldun see the translation of the Muqaddimah by Rosenthal (New

York, 1958) and also the *Histoire des Berbères et des dynasties musulmanes de l'Afrique septentrionale*, ed. de Slane (Algiers, 1847–51). An interpretation of his thought is provided by Muhsin Mahdi, *Ibn Khaldun's Philosophy of History* (London, 1957), which includes a scholarly bibliography.

The establishment of Ottoman rule and the period up to the French conquest have been relatively little studied, although much archival and other semi-primary material exists. Fernand Braudel, *La Méditerranée et le monde méditerranéen*, 2 vols. (Paris, 1966) is invaluable and has a comprehensive survey of primary and secondary sources. Sir Godfrey Fisher's *Barbary Legend* (Oxford, 1957) also has a valuable bibliography. P. Grandchamp, *La France en Tunisie, 1582–1620*, 3 vols. (Tunis, 1920–25) is a specialist work which gives an indication of the resources available in consular archives.

The establishment of the French protectorate has been studied by Jean Ganiage in *Les Origines du Protectorat français en Tunisie* (Paris, 1959), based on the diplomatic archives. More general works are S. H. Roberts, *The history of French colonial policy* (London, 1963) and Henri Brunschvig, *French Colonialism* (English edition, London, 1966). For the later period of French rule, see Roger le Tourneau, *Evolution politique de l'Afrique du Nord musulmane, 1920–1961* (Paris, 1962) and the sensitive collection of studies by Jacques Berque, *Le Maghreb entre deux guerres* (Paris, 1962), whose complex style is ably rendered into English by Jean Stewart under the title *French North Africa* (London, 1962). A brief account in English is Dwight L. Ling, *Tunisia from Protectorate to Republic* (Bloomington, 1967). Taalbi's *La Tunisie Martyre* was published anonymously in Paris in 1920.

The approach and achievement of independence provoked a number of short studies of the country which survey the history of the nationalist movement, of which the most stimulating are Salah-Eddine Tlatli, *Tunisie nouvelle* (Tunis, 1957), A. Basset and others, *Initiation à la Tunisie* (Paris, 1950) and a Marxist account (which includes much reliable information) by Paul Sebag, *La Tunisie* (Paris, 1951). The intellectual background to Tunisian reform is studied by Albert Hourani in *Arabic Thought in the Liberal Age, 1798–1939* (London, 1967). A specialist study of the Jewish community is André Chouraqui, *Marche vers l'Occident, Les juifs de l'Afrique du Nord* (Paris, 1952). An excellent study in English of the growth of the nationalist movement is the still unpublished thesis of Leon Carl Brown, *Tunisia under the French Protectorate: a study of ideological change* (Harvard, 1962), part of which is incorporated into: Charles Micaud with Leon Carl Brown and Clement Henry Moore, *Tunisia, the Politics of Modernization* (London, 1964).

Since independence Tunisia has attracted the attention of American scholars, and an excellent study of the politics of the country is to be found in Clement Henry Moore, *Tunisia since Independence* (Berkeley and Los Angeles, 1965), which contains a valuable bibliographical essay. Equally perceptive is Charles F. Gallagher, *The United States and North Africa* (Cambridge, Mass., 1964). William Zartman. *Government and Politics in Northern Africa* (New York, 1963) is reliable and succinct, though limited both in length and the period it covers. The researches of a Swedish political scientist are recorded in Lars Rudebeck, *Party and People* (Stockholm, 1967). Willard Beling, *Modernization and African Labor, a Tunisian Case Study* (New York, 1965) has useful information about the history of the labour movement. David Gordon's *North Africa's French Legacy* (Cambridge, Mass., 1965) is also useful, although it is not confined to Tunisia.

For studies of Bourguiba see Jean Lacouture, *Cinq hommes de la France* (Paris, 1961) and the record of interviews by Roger Stéphane, *La Tunisie de Bourguiba* (Paris, 1958). Bourguiba's view of the world and his career can best be studied from his own speeches and articles. The former have been published since 1956 by the Tunisian Ministry of Information; the latter are published in part by the Centre de Documentation Nationale in the series *Histoire du Mouvement national* under the title *Articles de Presse* (Tunis, n.d.). See also in this series *Le 'procès' Bourguiba 9 avril 1938* (Tunis, 1967).

Accounts of the economic development of Tunisia inevitably pass out of date with depressing rapidity, and can best be followed in the periodical literature (see below). The government's own plans and statistics provide valuable basic material – see especially the *Perspectives décennales* and the *Plan quadriennal*. The most useful surveys are in René Gallissot, *L'Economie de l'Afrique du Nord* (Paris, 1961), Moncef Guen, *La Tunisie indépendante face à son économie* (Tunis, 1961) and André Tiano, *Le Maghreb entre les mythes* (Paris, 1967).

Social change occurs more slowly than economic, and calls for longer study on the ground. Valuable contributions in this respect have been made by Salah-Eddine Tlatli in *Djerba, l'île des lotophages* (Tunis, 1967); Pierre Bardin, *La vie d'un Douar* (Paris and The Hague, 1965) which studies a hamlet in the Medjerda valley; Jean Duvignaud, *Chebika*, a village in the south; and André Demeersman, *La famille tunisienne* (Tunis, 1967). Valuable, too, for the questions it provokes about Tunisia, is the brilliant and perceptive comparison which Clifford Geertz makes between Indonesia and Morocco in *Islam Observed* (New Haven, 1968).

Periodical literature of Tunisian and French origin provides an outlet for new research and a reliable source of information on recent developments. *Cahiers de Tunisie*, published by the University of Tunis, and *IBLA*, published by the

White Fathers' Institut de Belles Lettres Arabes, both contain scholarly articles ranging over the whole of Tunisian history. The Centre d'Etudes et de Recherches Economiques et Sociales, part of the University of Tunis, publishes the *Revue Tunisienne de Sciences Sociales*. In France, La Documentation française publishes a quarterly documentary record entitled *Maghreb* while the Centre de Recherches sur l'Afrique Méditerranéenne at Aix-en-Provence publishes an invaluable *Annuaire de l'Afrique du Nord*.

Who's Who

ACHOUR, Habib. Popular trade unionist, having only technical-secondary education. Assisted Ferhat Hached in UGTT organization in Sfax, where he took a prominent part in the UGTT general strike of 5 August 1947. Was under arrest when Hached was assassinated. Led breakaway union (Union des Travailleurs Tunisiens) in conflict with Ahmed ben Salah in 1956. The UTT was reintegrated in 1957 and Habib Achour was co-opted to the Political Bureau of the Néo-Destour Party. In 1965 was himself ousted from the UGTT and expelled from the party in conflict with the government, in which ben Salah was responsible for the national economy. Arrested, convicted on ferry-boat charges March 1966, imprisoned but released in June. Reintegrated into the party, July 1967.

BEN AMMAR, Tahar. Independent notable, landowner who played an im-portant role in the transition to independence; formed a government, 1954, which negotiated the Conventions with France, and a second government to arrange elections to a constituent assembly, after which he resigned. Tried, irregularly, in 1959 and condemned; rehabilitated in 1969.

BEN SALAH, Ahmed. Born 13 January 1926 at Moknine. Educated at Sadiki College and in Paris, where he became general secretary of the Néo-Destour student branch. Took his *license* in Arabic literature in 1948 and began teaching at the lycée in Sousse. Joined the civil servants' trade union and headed the party branch at Moknine. Became General Secretary of the UGTT in 1954, but was ousted in a conflict with Bourguiba in 1956. Secretary of State for Public Health and Social Affairs, 1957–61. Appointed Secretary of State for the Plan and Finance, later National Economy, 1961–69 and in this office responsible for the direction of the Tunisian economy and for the development of co-opera-tives. In 1968 he was given in addition the post of Secretary of State for Education. In September 1969 he gave up the Ministry of National Economy and in November the Secretaryship for Education.

BEN YAHMED, Bechir. Director of the semi-official newspaper *L'Action* (established in 1955) and, at twenty-seven, Minister of Information in Bour-guiba's first government. Supported Bourguiba against Ben Youssef, but took an independent and critical line which resulted in the newspaper being closed in September 1958. In October 1960, ben Yahmed became director of *Afrique-Action*, the predecessor of *Jeune-Afrique* (since November 1961).

BEN YOUSSEF, Salah. Born 1910 in Djerba, joined the Néo-Destour and became a close collaborator of Bourguiba, who appointed him to the Political Bureau in 1937. He became General Secretary and controlled the party in Bourguiba's absence from 1945–49. In 1950 served as Minister of Justice (duly authorized by the Party) in the Chenik government. Left Tunisia in 1952 and was virtually in exile in Cairo. In 1955 he opposed the Conventions with France and expressed a pan-Arab viewpoint which enhanced his personal rivalry with Bourguiba. He returned to Tunis in September 1955, but was expelled from the party the following month. He took the battle into the country, where he enjoyed a considerable following. In January 1956 a major police operation brought 120 arrests and ben Youssef's flight to Tripoli, although the last of his followers, in Matmata, had still to be suppressed by the French. He was condemned to death in absentia, and assassinated in 1961.

BOURGUIBA, Habib. President of Tunisia. Born 1903 in Monastir, educated Sadiki College (Tunis) and Paris (Ecole libre des sciences politiques); joined Destour party 1921. Returned to Tunis in 1927 to work in a law office; soon engaged in journalism and politics. One of the founders of the Néo-Destour party in 1934. Imprisoned 1934–36 and 1938–43; travelled in the Middle East 1945–49 and made world tour in 1951; arrested 1952 and kept in confinement or under surveillance until 1955. Returned to Tunis after Franco-Tunisian Conventions of 1955; succeeded ben Ammar as prime minister after first elections; President of the Republic since 1957 and President of the Socialist-Destour party.

BOURGUIBA, Habib, Jr. Son of President Bourguiba, b. 1927, educated in Tunis and Paris. Counsellor, Tunisian Embassy in Washington, 1956–57, Ambassador to Italy 1957–58, to France 1958–60, to US 1961–63; Secretary of State for Foreign Affairs since 1964.

HACHED, Ferhat. Lorry driver from Sousse who became militant trade-union leader in Sfax, where in 1944 he led a group of unions out of the CGT, which was dominated by the French communists. He was not at this time a member of the Néo-Destour, but readily worked with party militants to form, in January 1946, the independent Union Générale des Travailleurs Tunisiens. The Union remained in existence when the Néo-Destour was suppressed in 1952 and Hached was of key importance until his assassination in December.

LADGHAM, Bahi. Born 10 January 1913 at Tunis, educated Sadiki College; civil servant under the protectorate but politically active with the Néo-Destour. Imprisoned 1940–44. Secretary of State to the Presidency since 1957, Secretary of State for Defence in 1964 and again after Ahmed Mestiri's resignation in 1968. Appointed General Secretary of the Néo-Destour party and member of the Political Bureau in 1955. Has been popular and trusted in the Party, and Bourguiba has relied on him for administrative co-ordination. September 1969, given wider powers of co-ordination which appeared to designate him as Bourguiba's successor. November 1969, appointed prime minister.

MASMOUDI, Mohamed. Born 1921 in Mahdia, educated Sadiki College (where he was a contemporary of Ben Salah and Taieb Mehiri) and Paris. A close friend of Bourguiba, he represented him abroad, and took part in the negotiation of the 1955 Conventions as a member of the ben Ammar governments. After independence was appointed Ambassador to France (1956–58). Removed from the Political Bureau in 1958 for support of L'Action's criticism of the régime, but reintegrated four months later and appointed Minister of Information. Again disgraced for his support of L'Action in 1961, but in 1965 reappointed Ambassador to France, to restore relations after the break of 1964.

MATERI, Mahmoud. One of the founders of the Néo-Destour party, and its first president. He came from an impoverished baldi family; educated in France where for a time he was an active communist, and came into contact with Bourguiba. He left the Communist party before his return to Tunisia. In 1938 he resigned from the presidency of the party in disagreement with Bourguiba's policy of violence, and after independence again criticized the degree of control practised by the party in elections. He was himself elected an independent member of the Assembly.

MESTIRI, Ahmed. Born La Marsa July 1925, coming from a petit bourgeois family, Destour supporters. Educated at the Lycée Carnot (Tunis), Algiers and

Paris: entered the bar in Tunis 1948. Active in La Marsa cell of the Néo- Destour. *Chef de cabinet* to Mongi Slim in Tahar ben Ammar's governments, 1954–55. Secretary of State for Justice in Bourguiba's first government. Secretary of State for Finance and Commerce, then ambassador to Moscow (1960), Cairo (1961) and Algiers (1962). 1966 Secretary of State for Defence, but resigned in 1968 over the speed of the development of co-operatives.

SLIM, Mongi (1908–69). Came from a family of lawyers. Joined the Néo- Destour and was co-opted to the Political Bureau, 1936. Responsible for negotia- tions with France, 1951–55. Sent as Ambassador to US and Canada and Delegate to UN, where he became President of the General Assembly 1961–62 (during the Congo crisis). Foreign Minister, 1962–64, the President's personal representative 1964–66, Secretary of State for Justice 1966–69.

SLIM, Taieb. Brother of Mongi Slim, born January 1914, educated at the Lycée Carnot (Tunis) and in Paris. Assistant Secretary N. African students in Paris. Condemned to prison in 1942, but released. Conducted propaganda in the Middle East, India and Pakistan (condemned to death in his absence). May 1956–62 Ambassador to Britain, then Permanent Representative to UN 1962–67. Personal representative of the President since 1967.

TLILI, Ahmed. Key figure in the relation between the trade-union movement and the Néo-Destour. Important in clandestine activity, particularly in enlist- ment of tribesmen in the Gafsa area in the last years of the protectorate, as a result of which he was appointed treasurer of the party and a member of the Political Bureau in 1955. Became secretary of the UGTT in 1957 and healed the rift between the union and the party following the dispute with Ben Salah. Removed from the Secretaryship in 1963 and in the fresh dispute with the party and government pleaded the case of the UGTT at the International Congress of Free Trade Unions in Amsterdam. Deprived of office and expelled from the party in 1965, he remained abroad until 1967 when he returned to make his peace with Bourguiba, and died.

Index

economic development, 165–6, 178, 186–202; agriculture, 166, 193–6, 197, 201; industry, 191–2, 200–1; trade, 173–4
education, 11, 181; during French protectorate, 118–22
El Djem, 8, 27, 29, *53*
El Habibia, 196
Elissa, Phoenician queen, 17
Eulj Ali, 78, 79, 80
Ewing report (U.N.), 172

FAISAL of Saudi Arabia, 183
family planning, 192–3
Farabi, 65
Fatimids, 46; in Egypt, 43, 45; over-lordship, 44
Fédération Nationale des Etudiants Destouriens, 158
Ferry, Jules, 118
Fez (Merinid capital), 48, 58, 61, 62
F.L.N. (National Liberation Front), Algeria, 169–70, 175
foreign aid, *see* economic aid
foreign policy, 167–85
France, *see* French Protectorate
French language, 11, 16, 102
French Protectorate, 10, 168–9; established, 91, 97, 98–9, 101–3, 120; Popular Front, 130; terminated, 133–5

GABÈS, 14, 128
Gambetta, Léon Michel, 101
Gaulle, Charles de, 91, 133, 176
Genseric, 33–4
Ghassani, Hassan ibn al- Nu'man al-, *see* Ibn al-Nu'man al-Ghassani, Hassan
Gordian, 26
Gregory (Byzantine ruler), 37

HAAKON THE OLD, 58
Hached, Ferhat, 132–3, 134, 135, 155, 156
Haddad, Tahar, 126–7
Hadrumetum, 23, 29; *see also* Sousse
Hafsids, 57–8, 68, 69, 70, 132; attacked by Merinids, 61–2, 63; collapse, 70, 74; restored by Charles V, 76, 77; by Don Juan, 78–9
Hamba, Ali Bach, 121, 122, 123
Hamouda Bey, 83
Hannibal, 20, 21; march on Rome, 22
Hanno, 25
Hassan, Abu al-, 48
Hassan ibn al-Nu'man al-Ghassani, *see* Ibn al-Nu'man al-Ghassani, Hassan
Hautecloque, Jean de, 134
Hilalian invasion, 46–7, 57
Himilco, 25
Histoire des Berbères (Ibn Khaldun), 65
Husain ibn Ali, *see* Ibn Ali, Husain
Husainids, 84, 90

IBN AGHLAB, IBRAHIM, 40
Ibn Ahmad, Ibrahim, 42
Ibn al-Khatib, 63
Ibn al-Nu'man al-Ghassani, Hassan, 38
Ibn Ali, Husain, 84
Ibn Ash'ash, 39
Ibn Hatim, Yazid, 40
Ibn Hudaij, Mu'awiya, 37
Ibn Imran, Ishaq, 42
Ibn Khaldun, 38, 46, 62–8, 71
Ibn Muljam, 39
Ibn Nafi, Uqba, 37, 38
Ibn Sa'd, 37
Ibn Sulaiman, Ishaq, 42
Ibn Tumart, 47
Ibrahim ibn Aghlab, 40
Ibrahim ibn Ahmad, 42
Ifriqiya, 70, 168
industry, *see* economic development
Ishaq ibn Imran, 42
Ishaq ibn Sulaiman, 42
Islam, *see* Muslim traditions
Islamic empire, *see* Muslim empire
Israel, *see* Arab–Israeli war

JERBA, ISLAND OF, 12, 17, 71, 199–201; attacked by Aragonese, 61, 68, 69; by Barbarossas, 75; by Draghut, 76, 77, 78; by Hafsids, 68–9; by Normans, 47; by Sicily, 70

Tamerlane, 64, 65
Tanzimat, 90
Tertullian, 27, 30, 100
TGM (railway), 8, 93, 98, 99
Thamer, Habib, 131
Thuburbo Majus, 27, 52
Tlemcen, 58, 62, 63, 69, 70
Tlili, Ahmed, 156, 157, 158, 163
Torrens Act, see Land Act
tourism, 201
trade, see economic development
trade-union movement, 126, 130, 132–3,
    150, 155–7, 158, 179
Treaty of Bardo, 101–2
Tripoli, 61, 68, 77
Tunis, 38, 58; British expedition
    (1655), 81–3; Great Mosque, 57;
    patron saint, 73; under Hafsids, 48,
    62, 63; Hapsburg overlordship, 76,
    78–9; Shi'ites, 45; riot in (9 April
    1938), 130; see also Zitouna Mosque
Tunis, University of, see University of
    Tunis
Turkish Empire, see Ottoman Empire

UBAID ALLAH, 43, 44
UGET, see Union Générale des
    Etudiants Tunisiens
UGTT, see Union Générale Tunisienne
    du Travail
Umayyads, 37, 39
Union Générale des Etudiants Tunisiens
    (UGET), 158–9
Union Générale Tunisienne du Travail
    (UGTT), 132–3, 155, 156

Union Tunisienne du Travail (UTT),
    156
United Nations Economic Commission,
    172–3
University of Tunis, 152, 154, 158
Utica, 18, 23
Utman, 70, 74

VALERIAN PERSECUTION, 30
Vandals, 33–5
Victor, bishop of Vita, 34
Viénot, Pierre, 130
Villet, Victor, 95, 96

WHITE FATHERS, 8, 100
women, status of, 13, 126–7, 129, 152
Wood, Richard, 92, 93, 95, 97–8, 99
World War I, 123
World War II, 131–2, 179

YAZID IBN HATIM, 40
Young Tunisians, 121–3, 124
Youssefism, 160, 170, 175, 177, 181;
    see also Ben Youssef, Salah

ZAGHOUAN, 27, 88, 93, 98
Zaouche, Abdel Jelil, 121
Ziri, 45
Zirids, 45, 46
Zitouna Mosque, 40; education at, 119,
    121, 152
Ziyadat Allah I, 42
Ziyadat Allah II, 42